LEAD SMART
in the AI ERA

Amit Kumar Jain, a seasoned author, columnist and civil servant with over 23 years of experience in public service, currently serves as the Director of Operations and Services at the Delhi Metro Rail Corporation (DMRC). He is known for spearheading the digital transformation within the DMRC, which is similar to his successful endeavours in digitalizing the freight business of Indian Railways. Dr Jain's expertise extends globally, having contributed to digital transformation strategies for entities like Iranian Railways in collaboration with the United Nations Economic and Social Commission for Asia and the Pacific (UNESCAP). He is also an experienced trainer of digital and traditional leadership and serves as visiting faculty to teach leadership at the Lal Bahadur Shastri National Academy of Administration (LBSNAA), Indian Institutes of Technology (IITs), Indian Institutes of Management (IIM), Indian Railways Institute of Transport Management (IRITM), National Academy of Indian Railways (NAIR) and other institutions. He holds a PhD from the School of Planning and Architecture (SPA), Delhi, an MTech from IIT Delhi and a BE from IIT Roorkee. His leadership credentials include successfully handling the challenges and opportunities of the AI era, a theme he explores in his books.

Surbhi Jain, an accomplished author, columnist and civil servant, is currently the Joint Secretary in the Department of Economic Affairs, Ministry of Finance. She completed her postgraduation from the Delhi School of Economics and graduation from Lady Shri Ram College. She has diverse work experience across industry, commerce, agriculture and school education. She has been involved in promoting the digital management of data in India's education system. Notably, she contributed to designing economic policies that promote digitalization and the use of technology in the fields she worked in. Ms Jain's extensive writings reflect her adeptness at addressing digital leadership challenges and opportunities.

'Data and outcomes are critical for good governance in the digital age. *Lead Smart in the AI Era* is an essential guide for leaders who want to deliver in a world where change is the only constant. It combines strategic vision with practical advice, demonstrating how to embrace the challenges and seize the opportunities of digitalization.'

—**Amitabh Kant**
G20 Sherpa, Government of India, and
Former CEO, NITI Aayog

'If you are a leader in today's fast-paced digital world, this book is your guide. The authors articulate a vision for leadership that balances technology, culture and innovation. It is a comprehensive go-to resource for anyone looking to stay abreast and ahead in the AI era!'

—**Nandan Nilekani**
Co-Founder and Chairman, Infosys, and
Founding Chairman of UIDAI (Aadhaar)

LEAD SMART in the AI ERA

**AMIT KUMAR JAIN
SURBHI JAIN**

RUPA

Published by
Rupa Publications India Pvt. Ltd 2025
7/16, Ansari Road, Daryaganj
New Delhi 110002

Sales centres:
Bengaluru Chennai Hyderabad
Jaipur Kathmandu Kolkata
Mumbai Prayagraj

Text and Illustrations Copyright © Amit Kumar Jain 2025
Photographs courtesy: Amit Kumar Jain

Copyright of the photographs vests with the respective
photographer/copyright owner.

While every effort has been made to trace copyright holders and obtain
permission, this has not been possible in all cases; any omissions brought to
our attention will be remedied in future editions.

The views and opinions expressed in this book are the authors' own and the facts
are as reported by them, which have been verified to the extent possible, and the
publishers are not in any way liable for the same. They do not represent the views
of the Government of India or Indian Railways. The publisher has used its best
endeavours to ensure that URLs for external websites referred to in this book are
correct and active at the time of going to press. However, the publisher has no
responsibility for the websites and can make no guarantee that a site will remain
live or that the content is or will remain appropriate.

All rights reserved.
No part of this publication may be reproduced, transmitted or stored in a retrieval
system, in any form or by any means, electronic, mechanical, photocopying,
recording or otherwise, without the prior permission of the publisher.

P-ISBN: 978-93-6156-492-5
E-ISBN: 978-93-6156-460-4

Third impression 2025

10 9 8 7 6 5 4 3

The moral right of the authors have been asserted.

Printed in India

This book is sold subject to the condition that it shall not, by way of
trade or otherwise, be lent, resold, hired out or otherwise circulated,
without the publisher's prior consent, in any form of binding or
cover other than that in which it is published.

*To all business leaders
navigating the complexities of digitalization
and transforming challenges into opportunities
with resilience, innovation and determination*

Contents

Introduction   *ix*

1. Data: A New Factor of Production   1
2. Vision in the Digital World   11
3. Outcome-based Business Models   19
4. Measure, Monitor and Improve   30
5. Working with Machines: Augmented Intelligence   42
6. Wary of Biases in Data   61
7. Process Innovation   71
8. Change Leader: Agile and Adaptable   85
9. Coopetition: An Ecosystem Approach   95
10. Fake Information   104
11. Personalization: The 5th P of Marketing   116
12. The Safety of Humans   124
13. Fraud Detection and Prevention   131
14. Data Security   139
15. Emotional Intelligence   149
16. Horizontal Organizational Structure   156
17. The Future of Work: Work 5.0   164

18. Human Resource Management   172
19. Predictive Analytics and Demand Forecasting   184
20. Responsible AI   195
21. Data Quality and Governance   205
22. The Blue Screen Catastrophe   217
23. Digital Transformation   229

Afterword   242
Acknowledgements   245
References   246

Introduction

'Going digital is no longer an option, it is the default.'
—Natarajan Chandrasekaran

Navigating the Complexities of the Digital World

On 11 September 2001, a series of terrorist attacks rocked the United States (US). Members of the extremist group Al-Qaeda hijacked four commercial airplanes and used them as weapons to target significant landmarks. Two planes crashed into the Twin Towers of the World Trade Center in New York City, another struck the Pentagon in Arlington, Virginia, while the fourth crashed into a field in Shanksville, Pennsylvania. The first attack occurred at 8.46 a.m. ET, when Flight 11 hit the North Tower of the World Trade Center. These coordinated attacks led to the loss of 2,977 lives and caused extensive damage to the targeted buildings.

Following the initial impact, the authorities swiftly ordered the complete closure of North American airspace—an unprecedented move in the history of aviation in the US and Canada. The airspace remained shut for two days, until 13 September 2001, when it was deemed safe to reopen it. This tragic event marked the deadliest terrorist attack ever recorded.

Twenty-one years later, on 11 January 2023, US airspace had to be shut down again, but this time, it wasn't due to a terrorist attack. Instead, it was because of a malfunction in a vital software system called Notice to Air Missions (NOTAMs) managed by the Federal Aviation Authority (FAA). This system is crucial for informing pilots about potential risks, such as closed runways, equipment issues, weather conditions and temporary flight restrictions. Unlike the air traffic control system, which ensures safe distances between planes, NOTAMs focus on safety hazards for individual flights. Pilots are legally required to check NOTAMs before taking off to ensure they are aware of any potential risks.

The trouble with NOTAMs began around 2 a.m. ET when the system stopped sending notifications to pilots. As a precautionary measure, the FAA halted all domestic flights until 9 a.m. when the system came back online. This failure led to the cancellation of approximately 1,100 flights and delays for nearly 7,000 flights across the US. Initially, there were concerns that it might have been a cyberattack or ransomware incident, given the prevalence of such threats in the digital realm. However, the FAA later on clarified that there was no evidence of a cyberattack. The failure was caused by a corrupted data file damaged by the personnel who failed to follow procedures. As per media reports, people working for a contractor with the FAA seem to have introduced errors into the core data used on the NOTAMs system.[1] The files were changed despite rules prohibiting such changes on a live system.

The NOTAMs failure of 2023 that impacted millions of air travellers in the US is a striking example of the complexities and risks of the digital world we are living in. So much so that the impact of corrupted data files may be as pronounced as the biggest terrorist attack in US history.

Welcome to the complexities of the digital world. Let us explore the evolution of digitalization and how it is redefining leadership roles.

Digitalization and the Industrial Revolution

The adoption of technology is intertwined with the four phases of the Industrial Revolution, and the evolution of digitalization can be traced back to these pivotal moments in history. Each industrial revolution introduced new technologies that transformed the way we work and live. The First Industrial Revolution (1760–1870), powered by steam, laid the foundation for mechanization. The second (1870–1970) accelerated industrial growth using electricity and mass production. The third (1970–2000), marked by computers and automation, ushered in the digital age. Now, in the Fourth Industrial Revolution (2000 onwards), advanced digital technologies like artificial intelligence (AI), big data, blockchain and the internet of things (IoT), cloud computing, robotics, automation, 5G, and fintech are reshaping industries and societies to move towards an AI era (Figure 0.1). Digitalization, which encompasses the integration of these technologies into various aspects of life, is a key driver of this ongoing revolution. It helps automate, optimize and connect processes, paving the way for an efficient and interconnected world using advanced digital technologies. The Fourth Industrial Revolution is often called the 'AI Era', with AI symbolizing the broader range of advanced digital technologies driving this transformation, as mentioned above.

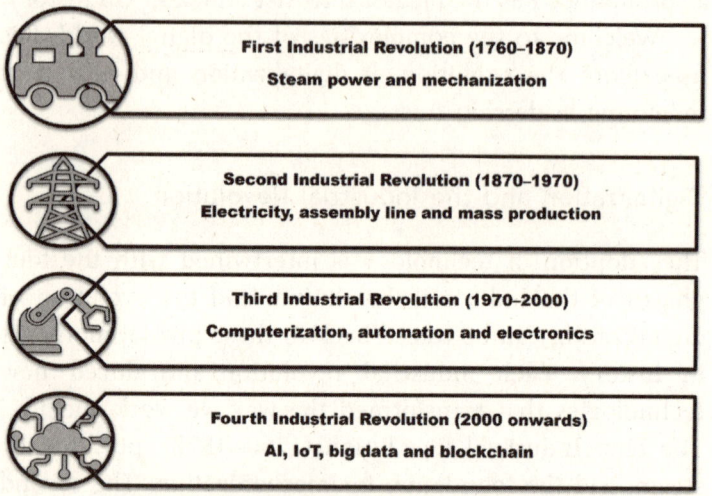

Figure 0.1: The four Industrial Revolutions

Digitalization boosts productivity but brings complexity and uncertainty. Leaders need to navigate extensive data, tech advancements and cybersecurity threats for success in the digital world.

The VUCA World and Leaders

Widespread digitalization has brought us into a different era marked by volatility, uncertainty, complexity and ambiguity or VUCA, a term commonly employed in business circles to depict the contemporary landscape shaped by the AI era. The term VUCA was first used by the U.S. Army War College to describe the post-Cold War world, but it has since been adopted by business leaders and academics to describe the complexity and rapid pace of change in all aspects of modern life (Figure 0.2).

V: Volatility refers to the rapid and unpredictable changes taking place in the world. These include economic fluctuations, political instability and rapid advancements in technology.

U: Uncertainty refers to the lack of predictability and the unknown. It is a state of being unable to anticipate or forecast what will happen in the future.

C: Complexity refers to the interconnectedness of systems and the many variables that come into play. It is a state of having many interconnected parts that interact in intricate and dynamic ways. In the context of digitalization, it means the interaction of technologies, data and human inputs that create complex, dynamic systems. These interactions, such as between algorithms, user behaviour and ethical considerations, influence decision-making and drive unpredictable outcomes.

A: Ambiguity refers to the state of having multiple possible meanings or interpretations. There is no clear or definite meaning. Ambiguity can make it difficult to understand a situation or make decisions.

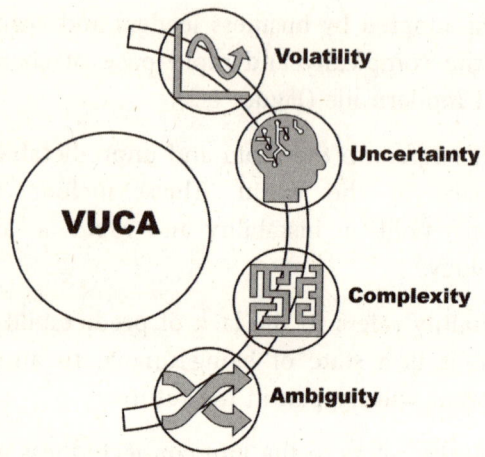

Figure 0.2: VUCA world

Leaders in a VUCA world that is driven by digitalization face formidable challenges. Volatility from rapid technological changes demands swift adaptability. Uncertainty requires informed decision-making. Complexity necessitates innovative problem-solving. Ambiguity needs to be dispelled through clear vision and communication. Thus, effective leaders requires agility, resilience, digital literacy and a proactive stance towards change.

Chat Generative Pre-trained Transformer's (ChatGPT) recent arrival in the ever-evolving digital sphere represents another transformative advancement in today's fast-paced and volatile world characterized by VUCA dynamics.

Advent of ChatGPT

In November 2022, OpenAI introduced ChatGPT to the

public. OpenAI is an AI research and deployment company based in the US. ChatGPT is an AI language model designed to engage in natural language conversations by providing responses based on vast amounts of pre-existing text data. It utilizes deep learning techniques to generate contextually relevant and coherent replies to user queries across various topics. Within a week of its launch, it had gained one million users due to its ability to write emails and essays, poetry, answer questions or generate lines of code based on a prompt. It quickly gained recognition for its capabilities, such as being able to pass the Wharton MBA and Minnesota University Law School exams. Within just four months (by March 2023), OpenAI announced the arrival of the upgraded version, ChatGPT-4. According to OpenAI, this next-generation language model is more advanced in three key areas: creativity, visual input and longer context. In terms of creativity, OpenAI says ChatGPT-4 is much better at creating and collaborating with users on creative projects. Examples of these include music, screenplays, technical writing and even learning a user's writing style. In November 2023, OpenAI indicated that it was actively working on ChatGPT-5, which promises a groundbreaking leap in natural language processing (NLP). Recognized for its human-like interaction, it is making waves in technology. Positioned to revolutionize human–machine communication, ChatGPT-5 is likely to include advanced problem-solving skills and an extensive knowledge base, thereby offering potential applications in various language-based tasks. ChatGPT-5 is likely to be released in 2025.

While ChatGPT serves to enhance people's effectiveness and efficiency, it is not immune to errors. A New York lawyer, Peter LoDuca, had to face a court hearing in 2023 after his colleague, Steven A. Schwartz, used ChatGPT for legal research.[2] The court discovered that the legal cases referenced in an ongoing lawsuit did not exist. Schwartz, a seasoned advocate, expressed regret and promised not to rely on AI for legal research without verifying the authenticity of the derived responses. The lawsuit involved a man suing an airline, and the airline's lawyers contested the legitimacy of the cited cases. This incident highlights the importance of verifying AI-generated information before using it.

Yes, the unbelievable, unimaginable and unthinkable has become the reality of our lives in the digital world. Digitalization has truly transformed the way we live, interact with each other, work, play and socialize. It is often claimed that the smart mobile phones in our pockets are powerful enough to put a man on the moon. A modern smartphone today is indeed much more advanced than the guidance computer used by NASA for the famous Apollo 11 mission in 1969.

Lead Smart in the AI Era Disrupted by VUCA

Successful smart leaders are ready to adapt their style to keep pace with the changing times. Today, digitalization led by AI has opened up numerous opportunities for businesses and individuals. Thus, contemporary leaders, too, should be ready to explore the new prospects that digitalization has made available. Traditional leadership traits include visionary thinking, the ability to inspire and motivate others, strong decision-making, the ability to build and lead a team, strong communication and interpersonal skills, emotional intelligence, adaptability, honesty and integrity, and a strong work ethic. Leaders in the AI era should possess many of the same traits as traditional leaders, but they also need additional skills and qualities to be effective in a rapidly evolving digital landscape. These could include the following:

- A strong understanding of and ability to leverage technology to drive business objectives and gain a competitive advantage.
- The ability to think strategically and anticipate changes in the digital landscape.
- Comfort with ambiguity and ability to navigate an ever-changing environment.
- Strong data analytics skills and the ability to make data-driven decisions.
- The ability to foster a culture of innovation and experimentation.
- Strong collaboration and networking skills to effectively work with cross-functional teams and partners.
- Strong digital communication and engagement skills to effectively connect with customers and stakeholders.
- Cybersecurity knowledge and the ability to protect the organization's data.

To summarize, leaders in the AI era should be agile, innovative and able to see how data, algorithms and AI open up new possibilities in an increasingly technology-intensive world. Today, the adoption of digitalization is not an option but a necessity. Darwin's theory of the survival of the fittest is applicable to the business world in terms of the survival of the business that is capable of adopting digitalization.

Challenges and Opportunities for Leaders in the AI Era

This book delves into the numerous challenges that leaders in the VUCA world encounter in the AI era, and offers insights on how to lead with smart strategies. The challenges include identifying valuable data, data cleaning, data mining, removing biases in data, safeguarding against fake data, issues of data governance, fast-changing business models, increasing competitive pressures, and so on. The organization structure, human resource management (HRM) and work culture need to be aligned with the new paradigm of working with machines and ever-increasing automation in the AI era. Further, online fraud, biases in models and data security are some offshoots of digitalization. The challenges and opportunities are two faces of the same coin. Challenges encourage innovation and create new opportunities. Unsurprisingly, many life-changing inventions were made due to existential challenges faced during the world wars. The first electronic computer, jet engine, radar and microwave oven were invented during the testing times of the world wars. The widely used antibiotic, penicillin, was the first antibiotic used to save soldiers from infections during the war. Likewise, the challenges posed by digitalization offer numerous businesses the opportunities to innovate, adapt and ultimately emerge stronger. This book further explores these opportunities brought about by digitalization to improve efficiency, increase market share, gain competitive advantages, delight customers and allow businesses to emerge as a market leader in the industry.

Organization of the Book

There are 23 chapters in this book, each dealing with specific challenges and associated opportunities. The last chapter presents a digital transformation framework, which indicates the steps involved in the digital transformation of an organization. The chapters illustrate how leaders may harness the power of data as a new factor of production while remaining wary of biases that could compromise its integrity. Visionary and smart leadership is essential for foreseeing changes and strategically positioning the organization for success amidst uncertainty. This vision drives the adoption of outcome-based business models, which focus on delivering value to customers and swiftly adapting to market demands. The opportunities for real-time measurement and monitoring ensure that leaders can identify areas of improvement and drive effective digital transformation. Embracing augmented intelligence facilitates organizations to work seamlessly with machines, thus enhancing human capabilities and decision-making processes. However, leaders must remain vigilant against the threat of fake data, and implement robust measures to ensure data authenticity and security. Personalization becomes paramount in marketing strategies to enhance customer experience in the AI era, and thus, ensuring the safety and well-being of employees and customers becomes a top priority. Detecting and preventing fraud in digital transactions is imperative for maintaining trust and reputation. Embracing emotional intelligence (EI) enables leaders to navigate complex interpersonal dynamics and foster a culture of agility and adaptability within their organizations. Collaboration and networking skills are essential for engaging with competitors for coopetition within complex digital ecosystems. A horizontal organizational structure facilitates agility and innovation, driving faster decision-making and process innovation. As work evolves, leaders must adapt HRM practices to attract, retain and develop talent in the AI era. Leveraging predictive analytics enables organizations to anticipate market trends and customer needs, driving informed decision-making. However, responsible AI deployment is crucial because of its societal impact and potential biases. Maintaining data quality and implementing robust governance frameworks are fundamental for leveraging data effectively while mitigating risks. A holistic approach to digital transformation encompasses changes in technology, processes and culture, thereby positioning organizations for success in an increasingly interconnected world.

In a world shaped by AI's rapid pace, this book offers a comprehensive guide for leaders to smartly navigate the VUCA landscape. From harnessing the power of data to fostering innovation and executing digital transformation, it provides invaluable insights to thrive amidst challenges and seize opportunities. Dive into its pages for a transformative journey.

'Being human in the digital world is about building a digital world for humans.'

—Andrew Keen

1
Data: A New Factor of Production

*'You can have data without information,
but you cannot have information without data.'*

—Daniel Keys Moran

Enigma machine used by Germans during World War II[1]

WARS ARE WON BY SOLDIERS WHO HAVE COURAGE AND A sense of duty; while some are forgotten, others are decorated with awards and medals. However, the list of unsung heroes includes innovators of military technologies. Many such technological developments in warfare frequently turned the tables during the six-year-long major global strife—World War II. In the early years of the war, the Axis powers, namely, Germany, Italy and Japan, had an advantage over the Allied powers, France, Great Britain, the US and the Soviet Union, because of the Axis powers' use of Enigma machines to transmit encrypted messages. The Enigma machine allowed for billions of ways to encode secret messages, making it almost impossible for enemy nations to decode the messages sent by the Germans. At this time, the United Kingdom (UK) was dependent upon supplies from the US and Canada to support its population and army. German submarines, called U-boats or undersea boats, often disrupted these supplies by sinking the ships from North America that carried essential provisions for the UK. It was understood that in the absence of any way to control these submarines, Britain would soon starve and fall in the war.

The encrypted messages transmitted through Enigma machines also included the locations of the U-boats. A keyboard was used to input the message, which was then encrypted before transmission. The machine was reset daily according to the code book, which had different codes for each day of the month. The encrypted message was then transmitted via Morse code to an Enigma operator at the receiver's location, where the message was decrypted by the Enigma machine using the same code for the day.

Britain soon realized that cracking the Enigma machines' codes was essential to gain an edge over the Germans. At the start of the war in September 1939, the UK deployed mathematician Alan Turing at the Government Code and Cypher School (GC&CS) at Bletchley Park—the top-secret nerve centre for code-breaking during the war. After months of hard work, in the spring of 1940, Turing introduced the prototype of his anti-Enigma 'Bombe'. His machine was able to use logic to decipher the encrypted messages produced by the Enigma machine.

As per war analysts, the Bombe machine, invented by Alan Turing and his team, helped end the war two years earlier than it would have ended otherwise, thus saving millions of lives and preventing unimaginable hardships. After the war ended in 1945, Turing joined the National Physical Laboratory (NPL) in London and started working on an electronic computer.[2] The Automatic Computing Engine (ACE) he designed was the first complete specification of an electronic stored-program all-purpose digital computer. He is considered the founding father of artificial intelligence and modern cognitive science.

Accurate and reliable information about the German submarines changed the course of World War II and proved to be instrumental in the victory of the Allied forces. History has witnessed many victories owing to correct and timely information and many defeats due to incorrect and misleading information. Indeed, misleading information was used as a tool to win wars. Information has been the most powerful weapon in winning wars for ages.

Information is nothing but data that collectively carry a logical meaning. Data have gained enormous importance in the AI era and are often referred to as the 'new oil' or 'new gold'. They are now an important factor of production—the building blocks of an economy. Traditional economists recognize four factors of production: land, labour, capital and entrepreneurship. Land includes all the natural resources such as water, oil, ores, natural gas, coal, forests, etc. Labour is the effort that people put into producing goods and services. Capital refers to the machinery, tools and buildings that labour uses to produce goods and services. Finally, the entrepreneur combines all these factors of production to generate profit.

Information derived from processing data has always been important for the efficiency and productivity of the other factors of production. For example, if you are a potter making earthen pots, you need certain information—the expected demand of the area served; your market share; the price after considering the price of similar pots offered by your competitors, how you can differentiate your product, and so on. Similarly, for a farmer, useful data for a better yield of crops include information about rainfall, soil moisture, fertility of the land, and the quality of seeds.

The traditional factors of production have been the root cause of most of the battles in the history of humankind. Control over these factors of production was the prime motive behind the conquests of Alexandra in the BC era and large-scale colonization in modern history. Again, data were extensively used in these battles to map the factors of production and plan winning strategies to exercise control over them. However, have we ever come across any battle in history that was fought to gain hegemony over data? We do not think so.

The relevance of land and labour has diminished significantly after the agricultural and industrial revolutions. The distinguishing factor that has gained prominence in recent years is access to data and the capability to process it effectively for growth. Data are the driving force for a platform-based economy, fuelling the growth of companies like Amazon, Uber, Airbnb, Facebook, X (formerly Twitter) and many more. Tom Goodwin, in his book *Digital Darwinism*, has aptly stated that 'Uber, the world's largest taxi company, owns no vehicles. Facebook, the world's most popular media owner, creates no content. Alibaba, the most valuable retailer, has no inventory. And Airbnb, the world's largest accommodation provider, owns no real estate. Something interesting is happening.'[3]

So, what do these tech giants have? The answer is volumes of data, both structured and unstructured, which they can harness to target their customers and run the most profitable businesses. The old saying 'knowledge is power' is gradually being replaced by 'data are power.' With the increasing importance of data, it would not be incorrect to say that data are emerging as a vital factor of production in the modern economy. An entrepreneur working from a small office in a remote location with a computer, access to the internet connection and data may run a profitable business depending upon how they use the data. The emergence of unicorns in India in the past couple of years demonstrates how data have empowered many of us to grow.

In 2020, the National Development and Reform Commission (NDRC) of China declared data as one of the factors of production. The NDRC stated, 'Today, new production factors such as data have a multiplier effect on the efficiency of other factors, forming advanced productive forces.'[4] Harnessing data in ways that create new insights and ideas is increasingly being done by data-driven applications that use a diverse set of data (spatial, documents, sensor, transactional, etc.) collected from multiple sources to help businesses make faster, more informed decisions. These applications are able to crunch large volumes of data using big data/AI/machine language (ML) technologies to present new insights. The analytic views provided by these data-driven applications are fuelled by the volume, velocity, variety and veracity of data available to an organization, which may significantly boost productivity. In a study conducted by the University of Texas, Austin, over 150 Fortune 1000 firms found that five attributes of data—quality, usability, intelligence, remote accessibility and sales mobility—have a dramatically positive effect on key financial measures.[5] The results of the study show that relatively small improvements in these attributes can pay off with big financial returns.

Unsurprisingly, tech giants have understood the value of data and are fiercely competing to gain access to more and more data. Amazon, Netflix, Airbnb, Facebook, X (erstwhile Twitter), etc. have become market leaders due to access to large volumes of data and their ability to productively use these data. Empowered by data, a new factor of production, these companies are daring to challenge the power of sovereign nations. In his book, *AI Superpowers*, Kai-Fu Lee describes a Wild West era wherein tech companies are free to battle for dominance with little government intervention.[6] This resembles European trading companies establishing their supremacy over sovereign nations during the Industrial Revolution.

Data colonialism is no longer a fancy word but a reality. It is the process by which governments, non-governmental organizations and corporations claim ownership of and privatize the data produced by their users and citizens. All the electronic devices (mobiles, tablets, computers, smart watches, IoT devices, etc.) that we use every day collect our personal data. The integration among these devices and pooling of our data create complete pictures of our personalities. Data colonialism is creating a new social order based on the real-time consumption of our personal data, which can be used by corporations for unprecedented opportunities of engendering social discrimination and behavioural influence. The collectors of our private data know more about us than we know about ourselves.

It is said that next-generation wars will not be fought on battlegrounds. Wars in a data-driven society will take place in a virtual space where fighting states will not capture each other's land but will try to capture data and compromise digital networks to inflict damage on the enemy. The ransomware attack on Colonial Pipeline in the US in May 2021, which halted all pipeline operations for around a week till the ransom was paid to the attackers, is an example of how data can become a new battleground among countries.

The biggest challenge for protecting data is its non-rivalrous nature, that is, the consumption of data by one doesn't affect the availability of the same data for another. The same data can be replicated multiple times, and millions of copies can be created. Unlike land or other assets, the owner of the data may not even be aware when confidential data has been stolen by the enemy.

In 2023, China tightened regulations on tech firms to control their use of vast data resources. Experts say these measures aim to rein in the power of tech giants, which previously thrived on unrestricted data collection.

Conclusively, in this VUCA world, the winning strategy for any entity will be to identify relevant data, clean them, mine them and use them to get a better insight into the business environment. Data need to be treated as an important factor of production, and like any other factor of production, they should be used efficiently to improve productivity and gain a competitive advantage. Data management and protection are the new competitive advantage an entity should strive for to gain market share.

Challenges and Opportunities for Leaders of the VUCA World

What data should I collect? How can it improve my organization's efficiency?

In today's fast-paced business environment, data are a valuable asset that can make or break an organization. Every organization generates a massive amount of data in its day-to-day operations, but the challenge lies in identifying these data and using them to create value for stakeholders. The task of mapping the data—what, where and how they are generated—falls upon the leaders of the organization.

The first step towards effectively utilizing data is to understand where they come from. Valuable data may not be limited to the organization but may also come from external sources such as weather reports, social media, competitors, stakeholders and the government. Once the data have been identified, they can be pooled for analysis, analytics and prediction to gain deep insights into the business. This, in turn, can lead to improved business performance in terms of productivity, profitability, efficiency, and customer and employee satisfaction.

However, using data to improve productivity is easier said than done. This is especially true for legacy organizations that have been slow to embrace digitalization. Employees may need to go against their natural inclinations to adapt to the new realities of the digital world.

The potential of data as a factor of production is limitless. The structured and unstructured data collected from various sources can be used to gain insights that were previously impossible to obtain. With the right tools and techniques, data can help leaders make informed decisions, improve customer experiences and create new revenue streams.

For example, a retail company can use data collected from its website and social media channels to gain insights into customer behaviour, preferences and buying patterns. These data can be used to personalize marketing campaigns and improve customer engagement, leading to increased sales and customer loyalty. Similarly, a manufacturing company can use data collected from sensors on their equipment to optimize production schedules and reduce downtime, resulting in increased productivity and profitability.

Conclusively, data are a valuable asset that, when properly identified and utilized, can significantly enhance an organization's performance and competitive advantage. Leaders must guide and encourage employees to embrace data as a new factor of production, unlocking its potential to drive productivity, profitability and customer satisfaction.

> *'Data really powers everything that we do.'*
> —Jeff Weiner

2

Vision in the Digital World

'Vision is the art of seeing what is invisible to others.'

—Jonathan Swift

IT WAS PERHAPS BEYOND ANYONE'S IMAGINATION THAT Steve Jobs, the founder of Apple Inc., visiting the Palo Alto Research Center (PARC), California, in December 1979 would forever alter the course of the development of personal computers.[1] The visit further pushed the Apple brand that was already leading the market.

Xerox Holding Corporation has ruled the photocopier market since 1959 when its engineers developed the first commercially viable copy machine. The patent for developing photocopying technologies and the consequent monopoly across America earned the company huge profits over the next decade. However, when the patent expired, Xerox faced stiff competition from various Japanese companies, including Canon. In the wake of new challenges, in 1970, Xerox decided to establish a research and development centre under the leadership of Jack Goldman. The purpose of this centre was, of course, to develop new technologies that would help maintain Xerox's leadership. Goldman created an environment wherein his team was encouraged to ideate, innovate, have freedom of thought, experiment and brainstorm to come up with new ideas. With such a conducive environment, PARC's innovative team sowed the seeds of many life-changing technologies, such as the computer mouse, ethernet networking and graphical user interface (GUI). Germination is a necessary but not sufficient condition for the seed to grow into a tree and bear fruit. Xerox's management was unable to foresee that these buds of technologies were capable of blossoming into huge opportunities. They perhaps did not want to invest in and support anything other than the successful business of photocopiers. Undeterred by the management's indifference, by March 1973, the PARC team had invented their path-breaking Xerox Alto. The machine incorporated a mouse and GUI a decade before mass-market GUI machines would become available. GUI allows a user to interact with the computer through graphic elements such as symbols, icons and buttons. Before GUI, the most common way to communicate with the computer was to write text commands in the command line interface. Users were required to remember numerous standard commands even for seemingly simple actions such as creating a file, opening, copying, moving, etc. GUI made interacting with computers so user-friendly that even a child can operate basic commands on a computer.

Xerox Alto: The first computer with a GUI and mouse, March 1973[2]

PARC gained its name for groundbreaking innovations across the world. Steve Jobs, the pioneer of the personal computer revolution, initially felt reluctant to visit PARC. However, he went there in December 1979. His words about the visit are reproduced below[3]:

> I had three or four people who kept bugging me that I ought to get my rear over to Xerox PARC and see what they were doing. And so, I finally did. I went over there. And they were very kind, and they showed me what they were working on. And they showed me really three things, but I was so blinded by the first one that I didn't even really see the other two. One

of the things they showed me was object-oriented programming. They showed me that, but I didn't even see that. The other one they showed me was really a network computer system. They had over a hundred Alto computers, all network using email, et cetera, et cetera. I didn't even see that.

I was so blinded by the first thing they showed me, which was the graphical user interface. I thought it was the best thing I'd ever seen in my life.

Now, remember, it was very flawed. What we saw was incomplete. They'd done a bunch of things wrong, but we didn't know that at the time. And still, though, the germ of the idea was there, and they'd done it very well. And within, you know, 10 minutes, it was obvious to me that all computers would work like this someday. It was obvious.

The rest is history. Apple introduced the desktop computer Lisa in January 1983. It was one of the first personal computers to offer the GUI in a machine aimed at individual business users. Apple Macintosh, introduced in January 1984, featured the GUI and first single-button mouse. In November 1983, Microsoft presented its GUI called Windows along with a mouse-based word processor called Microsoft Word at the Computer Dealers' Exposition (COMDEX).

The inventions by PARC researchers remained an academic feat until Steve Jobs envisioned the future of these technologies. This was not the first time that an invention remained buried for years, ignored despite its potential benefits and subsequent commercialization. Benjamin Franklin was credited with discovering electricity in 1752 when he conducted an experiment using a kite and key on a rainy day to demonstrate the relationship between lightning and electricity. Only after around 70 years of the discovery of electricity, Faraday invented the first electric motor in 1821. After another 58 years, Thomas Edison patented the first electric bulb in 1879. However, the twenty-first century is a different time. If a leader fails to envision the future, other visionaries will replace them. What Xerox leaders could not comprehend for years, Steve Jobs realized in a single visit. One of the PARC researchers who demonstrated the inventions to the Apple team led by Steve Jobs said, 'After an hour looking at demos, they understood our technology and what it meant more than any Xerox executive understood after years of showing it to them.'[4]

Uncertainty is inherent in the VUCA world, which makes it extremely challenging to visualize the future. In the twentieth century, we could still foresee what kind of life, education and career the next generation would have, but today, we are clueless. When we were engrossed in the virtual world created by social media, Mark Zuckerberg was envisioning its future and creating a new immersive virtual world—the metaverse.

Leaders of the VUCA world need to assess the far-reaching impacts of digital technologies on the market, competition, customer expectations, business processes, forward and backward linkages, end-to-end supply chains, and the industry ecosystem as a whole.

Challenges and Opportunities for Leaders of the VUCA World

What is my organization's 10-year vision? How can digital technologies help achieve it?

Although it is ideal to plan for the long haul, spanning 20–30 years, the rapid pace of change means that a vision extending beyond 10 years risks becoming outdated before it can be fully realized. This doesn't negate the importance of a long-term vision but emphasizes the need for flexibility in an ever-evolving digital landscape led by AI.

The organization's vision should be aligned with customers' burgeoning expectations in the AI era. Further, the vision should consider the emerging technologies that will impact the industry in the future. The legacy vision may have to be refined or redefined to take advantage of digital technologies, create new value for customers and become a market leader in the digital world.

Hyundai Motors, the well-known South Korean company, was founded in 1967. Since then, Hyundai has evolved to be a leading international car manufacturer. In 2019, Hyundai announced a new corporate campaign, 'Once Upon A Time, Hyundai was a Car Company'. This campaign highlighted Hyundai's transformation from an automobile brand to a smart mobility solutions company. The campaign aimed at consolidating the future of mobility with shared, connected and clean technologies.

In January 2022, during the Consumer Electronic Show (CES), Hyundai Motors shared its vision for robotics in the real world and metaverse under the theme Expanding

Human Reach to fulfil the unlimited freedom of mobility. The company is working to pioneer the new meta-mobility concept, going beyond physical movements through robotics and the metaverse to affect change in the real world. It envisions that distinctions among future mobilities will become blurred through extended robotics technologies such as AI and autonomous driving.

In the digital world, customers are unaware of the vast potential of emerging technologies. Henry Ford, the founder of Ford Motor Company, once said, 'If I had asked people what they wanted, they would have said faster horses.'

Similarly, the leader must infer what customers want, which may not be a straightforward answer.

Like Steve Jobs, Bill Gates and Hyundai, leaders could also envision the future and redefine their vision to suit netizens' expectations. The success of a company in the VUCA world depends upon its leaders' ability to see the future.

One key challenge for leaders is grasping the full potential of the latest convergence of digital technologies. Innovations like IoT, big data, AI/ML, robotics, cloud computing and 5G offer a wide array of applications. To harness these technologies for digital transformation, leaders need not necessarily understand the technical details, but they do need to stay informed about advancements in the digital space and beyond. This involves tracking the innovations happening across various companies, hiring consultants and seeking guidance from experts. Leaders must focus on what technology can achieve and then create a compelling vision to remain relevant in the AI era. By combining a technology-driven outlook with strategic digital initiatives, leaders can ensure success in this evolving landscape.

'Vision with action makes a powerful reality.'

—Ron Kaufman

3

Outcome-based Business Models

*'People don't want to buy a quarter-inch drill,
they want a quarter-inch hole.'*

—Professor Theodore Levitt

THE MESSAGE IS LOUD AND CLEAR THAT BUSINESS LEADERS need to focus on what customers actually want. When one buys a car, he actually wants mobility. When one buys an air conditioner (AC), he buys comfort. People are not interested in the product, but they look for the outcome. The user-friendly technologies, easy-to-use portals, IoT devices and mobile/web applications have made it easy to offer the outcomes of a product as services. Product-based business models are being transformed into service-based business models by leveraging digital tools. The concept of buying a product is now giving way to buying a service for the fulfilment of wants.

The sooner one realizes this, the better it is. Rolls-Royce is among the world's largest makers of aircraft engines. The company was established in 1904, and today it designs, manufactures and distributes power systems for aviation as well as various other industries. Rolls-Royce aero engines are widely used by Boeing, Airbus and Tupolev aircraft. Most aero engine manufacturers make a major portion of their money not only from the sale of new engines to aircraft operators but also from the engine's aftermarket support. In the late 1990s, Rolls-Royce decided to introduce a paradigm shift in the after-sales services they provided for its aero engines. It introduced the TotalCare maintenance programme whereby the customer (airline) was charged a fixed amount per flying hour for the aircraft engines provided by Rolls-Royce. Customers who opted for this program paid only for the engine that performed. The customer could avail reliable access to aircraft engines on a 10-year subscription basis without the need to stockpile spare parts or suffer disruptions during breakdowns.

Lesley So, Head of Marketing (Services) at Rolls-Royce, explained to *Le Journal De L'Aviation* in 2017[1]:

> We transformed the world of engine OEM 20 years ago when we introduced TotalCare. We turned the market upside down as we truly aligned our business model to that of our customers: in the past, engine OEM was making money when the engine broke and therefore needed to be fixed. The previous model is called the break–fix model. How we completely upside-down the model: we said, 'Actually we stand behind the quality and the reliability of the engine and airlines pay a rate per engine flying hour; we take away the complete cost maintenance and there's a risk transfer.' So, we're then completely aligned with our customer being satisfied to keep the engine flying as long as possible.

This has been successful due to the predictive maintenance

of engines based on the real-time data generated from an array of sensors installed on the engines. The Operational Service Desk in Derby, Kansas, USA, monitors real-time information on all Rolls-Royce engines around the world. The Rolls-Royce case is an example of how a typical product-based business model has transformed successfully into an outcome-based business model with the confluence of emerging technologies: predictive maintenance, IoT, AI/ML and cloud computing.

Mobility-as-a-Service

If stories are to be believed, the idea for Uber emerged on a snowy night in Paris in December 2008. Two friends, Travis Kalanick and Garrett Camp, were caught in a huge snowstorm in Paris. They were attending LeWeb, an annual European tech conference, where they were looking for business opportunities to invest the money they had recently earned by selling their start-ups for huge profits. Kalanick had received $20 million by selling his start-up Red Swoosh, a content delivery company, to Akamai Technologies. Camp had sold his company StumbleUpon, a web discovery engine, to eBay for $75 million the previous year. The duo could visualize the need for a technology-driven taxi service thanks to the inconvenience they faced on that snowy night. They decided to address the problem with a simple yet revolutionary idea of pushing a button and getting a car; thus, the famous mobile application, Uber, was developed.

In March 2009, Uber was founded as UberCab, a ride-sharing company, by Garrett Camp, Oscar Salazar and Conrad Whelan, with Kalanick serving as an adviser. The company quickly grew to become the world's most valuable start-up. Its success is attributed to its deep understanding of customers' needs and leveraging digital technology to deliver an efficient and hassle-free travel experience to them. It gained popularity over the years and has become the one-stop mobility solution for many people. As of May 2024, Uber has a large base of over 149 million monthly active users.[2]

How did Uber transform the vehicle hiring business? Uber's unique idea to connect service suppliers (taxi drivers) with customers through a digital platform disrupted the age-old business model of a taxi/vehicle-hiring business.

Similarly, shared mobility tries to create an environment of unlimited access to safe and convenient transportation for everyone by investing in mobility services such as car sharing and car hailing. The connected mobility solution envisaged a digital solution to link an individual's car with other cars, their office and more. Clean mobility entailed the introduction of electric vehicles including hybrid electric vehicles and fuel cell electric vehicles.

Like Uber, many other companies are offering mobility-as-a-service (MaaS). Simple calculations confirm that owning a car isn't financially wise if usage is not adequate due to high costs like purchase, fuel, parking, insurance and taxes. Hiring taxis or using ride-sharing services can be more economical as they eliminate fixed ownership expenses. This trend reflects a shift from product ownership to outcome-based models, where the focus is on obtaining the desired result—mobility—without the burdens of ownership. MaaS is a deviation from owning personal vehicles to adopting public transportation, using rental car companies and private ride-share transportation (such as Uber, Ola and BluSmart).

Outcome-based IT Services

The IT industry is increasingly embracing outcome-based business models. A significant barrier to adopting IT systems has traditionally been the substantial capital investment needed for data centre hardware. However, this trend is shifting with cloud service providers offering hardware-as-a-service models, hence reducing the need for upfront investments. Cloud services as a substitute for costly hardware are available in various formats, as explained in Box 3.0.

BOX 3.0 Cloud Computing Models

Cloud computing is the best example of providing solutions for need fulfilment rather than selling a physical product. Cloud computing is the on-demand delivery of IT resources over the internet with a pay-per-use pricing model. Users need not buy, own or maintain physical data centres and servers. They can access IT services, such as computing power, storage and databases, on an as-needed basis through a cloud service provider. The three most common types of cloud computing services are infrastructure-as-a-service (IaaS), platform-as-a-service (PaaS) and software-as-a-service (SaaS).

Infrastructure-as-a-service

Also known as hardware-as-a-service (HaaS), IaaS is computing infrastructure managed over the internet. IaaS or HaaS helps users

> avoid the cost and complexity of purchasing and managing physical servers. For example, if one only requires computing hardware as a service, the cloud service provider may offer virtual machines with specified configurations, such as storage and RAM. The user will have to load the operating system and other software on their own.
>
> **Platform-as-a-service**
>
> PaaS removes the need to manage underlying infrastructure (usually hardware and operating systems) and allows the user to focus on the deployment and management of required applications. A PaaS cloud computing platform is created for the programmer to develop, test, run and manage applications. For example, if one needs computing hardware with the operating system as a service, the cloud service provider may offer virtual machines with specified configurations and operating systems, like Windows, Linux and MacOS.
>
> **Software-as-a-service**
>
> SaaS provides the user with a complete product that is run and managed by the service provider. Also known as 'on-demand software', it is software in which the applications are hosted by a cloud service provider. Users can access these applications with the help of an internet connection and web browser. For example, if one wants a complete solution, including specified software, the cloud service provider may offer virtual machines, operating systems and software, such as Microsoft Office 365.

Deloitte, in an article titled 'Scaling XaaS-Outcome-based Monetization Models', reported that 'Based on industry trends we have tracked so far, providers have consciously been trying to craft customer-centric solutions to entice customers and sustain their loyalty via subscription models for their anything as a service (XaaS) offerings.' The outcome-based monetization solutions for XaaS are shown in Figure 3.1.[3]

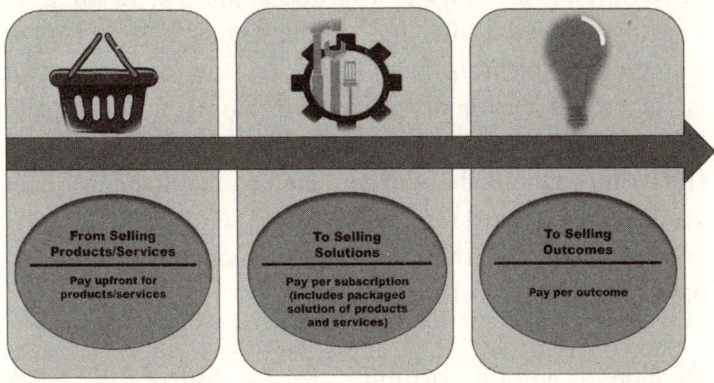

Figure 3.1: Outcome-based monetization solutions for XaaS

Outcome-based monetization models are focused on the result or outcome of the product/service and the value created from the product/service for the users. The user is required to pay only for the predefined tangible business outcome.

Train-as-a-Service

Considering the investment required to acquire new rolling stock, many rolling stock companies are innovating their business models to provide trains as a service. The service includes maintenance of the rolling stock for the duration of a contract and to an agreed upon service level. This model not only increases the scope and revenue potential for the operators but also enhances trust and longevity and fosters collaboration between the manufacturers and operators. The model is similar to the TotalCare solutions offered by Rolls-Royce for its aero engines. For example, in 2016, Hitachi Rail was awarded a contract to build 65 new high-speed trains for Virgin Trains in the United Kingdom. Hitachi is paid based on the outcome, that is, when its customers (UK train operators) complete journeys that meet predefined key performance indicators (KPIs) throughout the journey, such as maintenance, fleet availability, onboard temperature, and so on. Hitachi owns and maintains the trains, and the train operator in the UK pays Hitachi for on-time service.

Challenges and Opportunities for Leaders of the VUCA World

What do customers actually want? How can it be delivered as a service?

Leaders of the VUCA world need to develop a deep insight into what customers actually want. Do they want holes while the organization offers only drill machines? What outcome are customers looking for, and how can that outcome be delivered? The opportunities lie in offering what customers want and adopting an outcome-based model. The sooner one adopts an outcome-based model the better it is for gaining a competitive advantage. The market is full of examples wherein outcome-based business models have out-competed traditional product-based business models. Outcome-based models rely heavily on expected performance and high availability, which can be ensured through IoT-enabled, real-time monitoring, predictive maintenance, AI/ML tools and cloud computing. Leaders have to identify various XaaS business models and adopt a suitable one to remain ahead of their competitors. This business model also needs to be supported by digital technologies to ensure the delivery of outcomes as expected by customers and committed to by the service provider. Payments for the use of services can be linked to actual service consumption, which can be measured on a real-time basis through sensors and IT applications.

Steps for transforming a product into a service

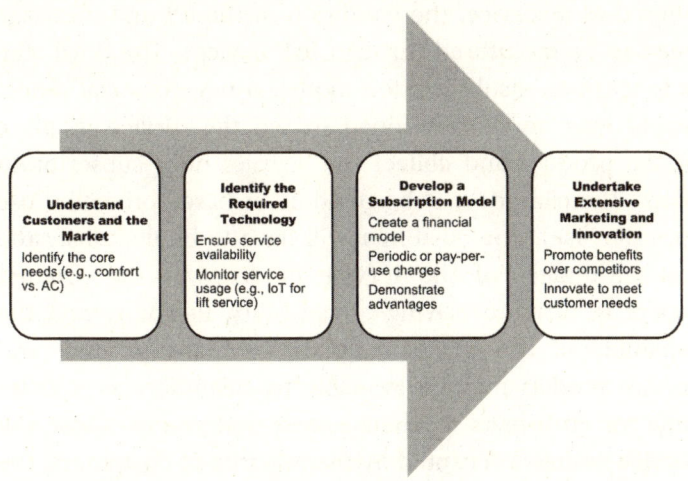

Figure 3.2: Steps for transforming a product into a service

The journey to convert a product into a service should start with knowing the customers and the market (Figure 3.2). What do customers want? What are their core needs; do they need an AC or the comfort of maintained temperature and humidity; do they want a refrigerator or a cool storage place for eatables; do they want a water purifier or safe drinking water; do they want a car or mobility service? Essentially, every product offers some kind of service, but it does not mean that every product can be offered as a service. Cars as a service (CaaS) in the form of a taxi have been available for years, but still people love to own cars. Thus, knowing the customer is the first step in turning a product into a service. The second step is to identify the technology required to ensure the availability of the service and monitor the use of the service. For example, if a lift is offered as a service, the condition of the lift and its usage need to be monitored through IoT devices. The third step is to work on a subscription model. A new financial model would have to be developed to sell the service in place of the product and collect the charges on a subscription basis. The charges may be periodic or based on actual use (pay per use). The customer will have to be demonstrated the advantages of the service model over the product model in terms of savings, availability, flexibility and the reliability of the service. Initially, both the product and service models may be available to customers as it takes time for customers to change their preferences. Once the service model is accepted by the majority of customers, the product model may be progressively withdrawn. The fourth step is conducting extensive marketing of the new model to illustrate its benefits and how it is better than that offered by the competitors. The next step is to keep innovating the service model to remain aligned with customers' needs and to stay ahead of the competitors.

For example, in many major India cities, ACs can now be rented on a monthly basis via a PaaS business model. Instead of purchasing an AC, customers can have the service provider install the unit in their homes; they then pay a monthly service charge that covers the cost of the AC and its maintenance. The service provider takes care of all the maintenance and servicing, while the customer is only responsible for electricity usage. This innovative approach shifts the traditional product-based model into a service-based model, which is designed to meet the customer's core need of cooling and humidity control without the long-term commitment or upkeep of owning an AC. Conclusively, converting the product into a service is easier said than done. Leaders of the VUCA world may find this transition overwhelming initially, but the sooner it is done the better it is.

> *'The best customer service is if the customer doesn't need to call you, doesn't need to talk to you. It just works.'*
>
> —Jeff Bezos

4

Measure, Monitor and Improve

> *'Measurement is the first step that leads to control and eventually to improvement. If you can't measure something, you can't understand it. If you can't understand it, you can't control it. If you can't control it, you can't improve it.'*
>
> —H. James Harrington

TRULY, THE THINGS THAT CANNOT BE MEASURED CANNOT be managed. An objective assessment of the outcome or performance of systems has been a challenge. For example, how was the quality of your sleep last night? How much did your customers like a particular dish served in the restaurant? How much was the customer satisfied with the response given by the call centre? And many more. Can these outcomes be measured objectively? Digitalization has created several new ways of measuring immeasurable data and managing the somewhat unmanageable opinions, emotions and other subjective factors through quantitative means. Some examples of such intelligent measuring systems are discussed in this chapter.

Attention Score

The famous sixteenth-century Chinese novel, *Journey to the West*, is a story about the legendary pilgrimage of a Tang dynasty Buddhist monk, Tang Sanzang, to India. The story, set in the seventh century, traces his journey. He is assigned the noble task of obtaining sacred Buddhist texts by Gautama Buddha. To aid him in his journey to India, the Buddha provides the monk with three protectors who agree to help him to atone for their sins. Sun Wukong, one of Gautama Buddha's disciples, accompanies Sanzang on this adventurous but torturous journey. Wukong is a monkey born from a stone and has acquired supernatural powers through Taoist practices. According to the legend, he was amazingly powerful and strong. He could lift two heavy mountains on his shoulders while running at the speed of a meteor. To control Wukong's possible unruly behaviour, an unremovable gold band was placed around his head and tightened with a magical incantation. With the tightening of the band, he would experience extreme agony despite his physical prowess. Thereafter, Wukong obeyed all of Sanzang's orders. After 14 years of arduous but successful journeys, Wukong and Sanzang achieved Buddhahood or nirvana.

Students of Jinhua Xiaoshun Primary School in eastern China compare their electronic headbands with the gold band used to tame the famous monkey king: Sun Wukong. *The Wall Street Journal*, in an article titled 'China's Efforts to Lead the Way in AI Start in Its Classrooms', reported that the students in this school are required to put headbands on their heads before class begins.[1] The electric signals generated from the brain's neurons are sensed by the headband to assess a student's level of concentration, which is measured in terms of attention score. A good attention score is indicative of higher concentration, which, in turn, leads to better performance by the student. A drop in the attention score indicates that the student's attention is waning. The software generates real-time alerts about students' attention level and also generates a report at the end of each class. These alerts are also sent to the parents to make them aware of their wards' concentration level in classes. The stated objective of this technology is to improve the level of concentration and the effectiveness of the learning process. Critics, however, frequently raise concerns about the infringement of students' privacy and the unnecessary psychological pressure on children due to such applications of these gadgets.

Headband used in China's classrooms[2]

Usage-based Insurance

The premium for a vehicle in traditional insurance systems is calculated according to the type of vehicle, its age, the age of the vehicle's owner, gender, type of coverage chosen and other quantifiable factors. However, insurance agents usually ignore important factors such as the actual running of the vehicle and whether the vehicle is driven rashly or carefully. Undoubtedly, the insurance cost should also account for the associated risks that increase with the use of the vehicle and the rash behaviour of the driver. Insurance agents are now using telematics devices. These devices offer cost-effective solutions to monitor actual risk and decide the insurance premium accordingly. Telematics-based insurance is a form of policy in which insurance companies rely on in-vehicle tracking devices to monitor the driving habits and risk-taking tendencies of the insured. The devices track the vehicle's speed, distance travelled, total driving time, braking, speeding up and other factors to help determine the policyholder's car insurance premiums. These usage-based insurance (UBI) policies usually come with a mobile app through which the insured can easily access real-time data showing their driving behaviour and, accordingly, varying rates of insurance premiums to be paid. UBI not only lowers the premium for responsible drivers but also prompts better driving behaviours, thus improving road safety. UBI has helped transform standard insurance products into a pay-per-use model or an insurance-as-a-service model. Evidently, the insured's behaviour was immeasurable till recently and is now becoming an objective criterion to assess the insurance premium with the help of digital technologies.

Continuous Glucose Monitoring System

According to the World Health Organization (WHO) website, about 422 million people worldwide have diabetes in 2024, with the majority living in low- and middle-income countries.[3] Diabetes accounts for 1.5 million deaths each year. The regular monitoring of blood glucose levels is vital to control this disease. The sugar level is usually measured through blood tests in the lab or blood glucose glucometer kits. However, it was impractical to continuously monitor a person's sugar level till the invention of continuous glucose monitoring (CGM). It is a sensor that can be implanted below the patient's skin. The sensor has the ability to measure a person's blood glucose level and transmit it to the associated mobile application. The app's interface presents readable data that can be monitored on a real-time basis by the person and their doctor. The system can generate an alert if the blood sugar level is not within the acceptable limit, and the necessary action, such as an insulin injection, may be taken. The continuous measurement of glucose levels has become very effective in managing diabetic conditions in patients.

Activity Tracker

IoT can help track a patient's activity to ensure that they are adhering to the treatment. Connected medical devices can track all vital parameters of the patient and encourage them to follow the treatment. Non-adherence to treatment is logged into the system, and an alert goes out to the doctor as well as the patient. The activity tracker can be in the form of a wristband or any other non-invasive device. So, the real-time measurement of a patient's activities helps manage their health plan.

Smart Irrigation System

More than half of the irrigation water is wasted due to runoff, wind and evaporation because most irrigation systems across the world rely on flooding farms with water after a scheduled interval so that water can reach every plant. The efficiency of irrigation can be increased by watering the crop only when needed and using exactly the right amount.

Smart irrigation systems make extensive use of IoT sensors. The sensors are placed in the field. They send real-time data regarding the level of moisture in the soil, weather conditions and plant water status to a cloud server for analysis. The system automatically switches on a water pump whenever moisture or temperature values are lower than the predetermined range. The real-time measurement of water through sensors helps improve the efficiency of the irrigation system.

Measure, Monitor and Improve

From the above examples, two distinguishing features of the AI era emerge clearly. The first is the ability to measure previously immeasurable parameters. Perhaps the sky is the limit when it comes to measuring something using digital devices. There are opportunities to deeply analyse business processes to identify the parameters that can be measured to improve the efficiency of the process and optimize cost. Digital devices may be installed on various components/equipment/machines to generate data that can be further processed and analysed to get deeper insights.

The second feature is the possibility of real-time measurement through digital devices. In the past, it was not feasible to have a cost-effective solution to continuously monitor essential parameters. The human-based system was not only costly but also prone to errors. Unsurprisingly, human errors are the single most common reason for road accidents. Thanks to large-scale digitalization, we create roughly 2.5 quintillion bytes of data every day. With the growing popularity of IoT, this data creation rate will only increase. We are living in an era where we have access to real-time data regarding our health parameters, condition of assets and traffic situation and can track and trace objects. Real-time data is paving the way for business analytics, predictive maintenance, demand forecasting and on-the-fly interventions.

Real-time data is also important for customers to improve their level of satisfaction, prevent fraud and keep themselves updated. For example, customers need to be alerted about any financial transaction in their bank accounts or debit/credit cards, their health parameters through smartwatches and other wearables, a security breach at home while they are away via a smart lock/CCTV, etc.

Measuring identified parameters is not sufficient in itself unless these are monitored effectively through digital visualization tools. Conventionally, data is measured and then presented in the form of tables and graphs and performance is assessed based on comparison with past data, like performance in the past quarter, past year, past decade, etc. Year over year, quarter over quarter and month-over-month are the most popular forms of comparison. The graphical way of presenting data has been observed to be the most powerful and effective because we are hardwired to see figures, pictures, images and graphical patterns even if they do not exist. You must have seen beautiful patterns in the clouds. Figure 4.1 is of the north face of Mount Kailash in the Himalayas, which I visited in 2011. I could visualize an image of a human face on the mountain. Indeed, our ability to visualize figures is a life-saving skill. In thick forests or high grasslands, we needed to identify predators from a distance or we would have become delicious food for some lucky predator. Even if there is no predator but some pattern resembling a predator, our first reaction is to run to save our lives. We have an innate ability to visualize graphical patterns, form a figure in our brains and identify danger to save our lives. So much so that most of the time we err on the side of caution when we visualize a figure by connecting some unrelated dots even if there is no such thing in reality. The human mind responds more to images and retains patterns better than numbers. That is why we are able to make more sense of graphs and pictures at first glance than of raw data and tables. Modern data visualization tools facilitate the presentation of data in visual form. By definition, data visualization tools are software applications that render information in a visual format, such as a graph, chart or heat map, for data analysis purposes. These digital tools make it easier for us to understand data and allow us to work with massive amounts of data. These tools are the best way to monitor the data needed to be measured to improve performance.

Figure 4.1: Human face on the north face of Mount Kailash, 2011

Data visualization tools also help find the most important parameters affecting performance. For example, if it is known that performance is affected by 10 parameters, data visualization tools can identify the parameters that affect performance the most. A leader can focus on these factors to improve performance rather than wasting resources on all parameters. A heat map is one such visualization technique that represents data graphically, where values are depicted by colour, making it easy to interpret complex data and understand them at a glance. Leaders can identify the parameters that need attention as well as the ones that can be safely ignored without any perceptible impact on performance.

Challenges and Opportunities for Leaders of the VUCA World

What new KPIs can digital technology measure? What real-time data is available? How can it improve performance?

In today's fast-paced business environment, leaders are constantly seeking new ways to improve the efficiency and performance of their organizations. With the advent of digital technologies, IoT devices, sensors and other cutting-edge technologies, leaders now have the ability to measure and monitor important parameters like never before. The challenge is to identify the new KPIs needed to measure the health and productivity of the organization and to use these insights to enhance customer satisfaction.

One of the most exciting opportunities presented by real-time monitoring is the ability to measure and monitor previously non-measurable elements. With the help of technology, leaders can monitor many parameters in real time to ensure timely intervention if required. For example, real-time monitoring of the movement and storage of packages in a warehouse can help optimize warehouse operations; real-time data from machines can be used for predictive maintenance; and real-time sales data from retailers can be used by manufacturers and suppliers for demand prediction and to ensure the prompt supply of products.

Real-time monitoring offers a host of benefits to organizations. By providing quick access to data and alerts, leaders can make timely decisions and increase business agility. The availability of assets can be improved through predictive maintenance, by reducing downtime, and by ensuring that the organization is always operating at peak efficiency. By leveraging data visualization tools, leaders can effectively monitor and manage KPIs, thereby making sense of complex data in an intuitive and easy-to-understand way.

Further, real-time monitoring facilitates the generation of alerts when important parameters breach acceptable ranges. For example, if a machine is not operating within its normal range, the system can generate an alert so that timely action can be taken to address the issue. Such real-time monitoring allows an organization to proactively address issues before they become larger problems, improving the organization's overall efficiency and effectiveness.

Real-time monitoring can also help organizations better understand their customers. By monitoring customer behaviour and preferences in real time, organizations can quickly identify trends and patterns and adjust their strategies accordingly. This can lead to improved customer satisfaction and loyalty as well as increased revenue and profitability.

For example, Real-Time Train Information System (RTIS) is a case of how IoT is being leveraged for the real-time monitoring of large-scale transportation networks like Indian Railways. The RTIS, developed by Indian Railways in partnership with Indian Space Research Organisation (ISRO), is a satellite-based solution for tracking trains in real time. The primary benefit of the RTIS is its ability to provide accurate, up-to-date information on train movements, leading to enhanced operational efficiency and safety. This system helps reduce delays, improve train punctuality and enable better resource allocation. Passengers benefit from real-time updates on train schedules and potential delays, improving their travel experience. Additionally, the RTIS contributes to streamlined train management in terms of optimizing track and platform usage, thereby facilitating smoother railway operations.

In conclusion, real-time monitoring presents a wealth of opportunities for leaders seeking to improve the efficiency and performance of their organizations. The possibilities are endless, and the potential benefits are enormous.

> *'The core advantage of data is that it tells you something about the world that you didn't know before.'*
>
> —Hilary Mason

5

Working with Machines: Augmented Intelligence

'You will be paid in the future based on how well you work with robots.'

—Kevin Kelly

THE CONCEPTS OF INTELLIGENT MACHINES AND AI CAME into being in the late 1960s. Since then, computer scientists worldwide have been working on improving the cognitive capabilities of so-called intelligent machines. To test the applied usage of AI, scientists experimented by teaching the computer, an intelligent machine, the game of chess. The game poses challenging problems for minds and machines but has simple rules, so it was thought to be perfect for such experiments. Over the years, numerous experiments were conducted on many chess masters and most AI-assisted computers failed. The decisive match between IBM Deep Blue and world grandmaster Garry Kasparov in 1997, however, changed history.

IBM computer scientists had been working to develop chess-playing software that could challenge the world champion. In 1989, IBM hired Feng-Hsiung Hsu and Murray

Campbell. Both were earlier associated with a project involving chess-playing machines while studying at Carnegie Mellon University. IBM named this project Deep Blue; it was aimed at developing the most advanced chess-playing machine. After conducting numerous trials, IBM decided to invite Garry Kasparov, the then world chess champion, to play with Deep Blue in 1996. The matches were held from 10 February to 17 February 1996, in Philadelphia, Pennsylvania. The first game was won by Deep Blue, the second by Garry, the third and fourth were drawn and fifth and sixth were won by Garry. Overall, Garry won the matches by a score of 4–2. Although Gary was the winner, this was the first time a computer had defeated a reigning world chess champion under normal chess tournament conditions.

Learning from these matches, the IBM team decided to double the system's speed to improve Deep Blue's performance.[1] A new chess chip was developed with the enhanced ability to evaluate the positions pawns can take. The new version of Deep Blue could search up to 200 million options per second depending on the pawns' positions on the board. The IBM scientists also enhanced Deep Blue's capabilities in terms of its ability to recognize and evaluate chess concepts, including positions and lines of attack. The machine could then look for possibilities and figure out the best move to win the game.

The IBM team re-invited Garry Kasparov in 1997 to play chess with the upgraded version of Deep Blue. The matches were played at the Equitable Center in New York. The game started on 3 May 1997. Moved by the 1996 match, millions worldwide were hooked to their television (TV) screens to see the outcome of the match between man and machine.

Garry won the first game, Deep Blue took the next one and the two players drew the three following games. Before the last (sixth) game, the overall score was even: 2½–2½. The last game, played on 11 May 1997, ended with an unbelievable defeat of Garry in barely 19 moves that lasted a little over an hour. The final score was Deep Blue vs Gary Kasparov at 3½–2½. The match marked a watershed moment for the relationship between man and machine when Deep Blue, equipped with AI, finally achieved what computer scientists had been claiming for decades. The match proved that AI-powered intelligent machines can even surpass humans with high-level cognitive abilities. Later, lots of funds poured in for more research programmes and developments in AI, which culminated in another windfall victory of machines over man. In 2016, Google DeepMind computer defeated Lee Sedol in the game of Go. Go is much more complex than chess.[2] There are 10^{360} moves possible in Go compared to the 10^{123} moves possible in chess. Sedol, known for his creativity and considered the greatest player of the previous decade, was an 18-time Go world champion at that time. According to him, 'In game two, the Google machine made a move that no human ever would.'

Garry Kasparov's defeat by Deep Blue in 1997 was not only a defining moment for AI development but also a life-changing moment for Garry. Instead of being resigned to his fate, he realized the potential of machines, and introduced a new form of chess in which humans and computers cooperate instead of contending with each other. In this, the human player uses a computer chess program to explore the possible results of one's moves and the possible moves by the opponent, as illustrated in Figure 5.1. This new game is known by different names: freestyle chess, centaur chess or cyborg chess.

Figure 5.1: Freestyle chess

'Weak human + machine + better process was superior to a strong computer alone and, more remarkably, superior to a strong human + machine + inferior process.'

—Garry Kasparov

Freestyle chess is a perfect example of how visionaries see the optimal interplay between humans and machines. Humans and computers do not approach the same task the same way. Humans are good at strategic guidance, whereas machines are lightning-fast at computations. Working together in playing chess produces a force that plays chess better than either humans or computers can manage on their own.

AI on the Board of Directors

Considering AI's capability to process and analyse vast amounts of data better than humans, Deep Knowledge Ventures (DKV), a venture capital firm in Hong Kong, made history in 2017 when it appointed Vital, the first AI robot, to the board of directors.

DKV is in the field of funding researchers working on developing new medications for diseases and illnesses for which no medicine is available. It is a highly risky business because 96 per cent of the drugs fail during trials. It is extremely difficult to select the right proposals, which have the potential to succeed, for funding. DKV decided not to make any positive investment decisions without Vital's approval. All applications are first scrutinized by Vital, and its recommendations are carefully thought out before deciding on any investment. As per DKV, Vital has helped them avoid many risky investments that could have bankrupted the company. This is a shining example of how the synergy between man and machine may tremendously enhance an organization's performance.

In February 2024, Abu Dhabi International Holding Company (IHC), valued at $238 billion, introduced an AI-powered observer, Aiden Insight, to its board to enhance decision-making processes.[3] Aiden Insight will leverage its capability to instantly analyse extensive business data spanning decades, market trends, global economic indicators and financial information. Aiden, derived from Irish roots meaning little fire or fiery one, signifies AI's potential to spark innovation. Its surname, Insight, underscores its profound data analysis skills and its role in providing the board with valuable perspectives. Aiden Insight will serve as a non-voting observer during IHC board meetings. It is tasked with compliance monitoring and risk assessment, which encapsulate its symbolic meaning and functional purpose in its board observer role.

Machines Can Outperform Human Doctors

As per the findings published in the journal *Nature* in 2020, AI powered by Google's DeepMind algorithm is capable of reading mammograms, X-rays commonly used to check for breast cancer, more accurately than human doctors, and successfully detect breast cancer.[4] The AI system reduced false positives by 5.7 per cent. False positive means when a patient is diagnosed wrongly with the disease. The findings also reduced false negatives by 9.4 per cent, meaning it caught instances of cancer that would have otherwise gone undetected. This significant improvement in diagnosis could benefit millions in terms of early detection of the disease and timely medication, thus saving many lives. Unlike humans who can assess a few thousand X-ray scans in their lifetime, machines can go through millions of scans in a matter of days. Currently, one of the biggest uses of AI in the medical field is to assist in image analysis. For X-ray images, ultrasounds, magnetic resonance imaging (MRIs), positron emission tomography (PET), and computerized tomography (CT) scans, AI can be used for the first level of scanning and suggest the findings to human doctors. The doctor takes the final call on the detection of the disease, further diagnosis and medication. AI augments the capabilities of human doctors to make them more effective and accurate.

Leveraging AI for Diabetic Retinopathy Screening in India

The impact of AI on screening for diabetic retinopathy (DR) in India can be significant, particularly in addressing the challenges posed by the large diabetic population and shortage of ophthalmologists in the country. DR is a leading cause of blindness among adults, and early detection is crucial for the effective management and prevention of vision loss. A study concluded that the automated AI analysis of retinal imaging can be used as an initial tool for mass retinal screening in people with diabetes.[5] In October 2023, Rajan Eye Care Hospital in Chennai launched a project to diagnose DR and glaucoma among the city's slum dwellers.[6] The project uses AI for retinal image analysis to treat DR and macular degeneration. AI algorithms facilitate early intervention and improve patient outcomes.

Agri Drones to Augment the Intelligence of Farmers

For centuries, agriculture has relied heavily on manual labour, with farmers managing every aspect from planting to selling. Despite its apparent simplicity, farming is a multifaceted endeavour vulnerable to factors like weather, soil conditions and labour shortages. Traditionally, monitoring crops has depended on human intelligence but is often limited by the vastness of farms and shortage of skilled labour coupled with rising wages. However, AI-driven solutions, particularly drones, are revolutionizing agriculture by offering a multitude of benefits such as crop monitoring, field mapping and precision agriculture.

Equipped with advanced cameras and sensors, drones provide real-time data on crop health, soil conditions and environmental factors. These data enable farmers to make informed decisions regarding resource allocation—including the precise spraying of pesticides and fertilizers and targeted irrigation—and livestock monitoring. Additionally, drones facilitate early disease detection, thereby optimizing farming practices, enhancing yield estimation and minimizing risks. Consequently, they promote sustainable and efficient agriculture while reducing environmental impact.

Recognizing the potential of drones in agriculture, the Indian government has taken proactive measures to promote their use. Initiatives such as the standard operating procedure (SOP) for drone application, launched in December 2021, have facilitated the widespread deployment of drones for tasks like pesticide and fertilizer spraying. This has proven to be more cost-effective and efficient than traditional methods.

Furthermore, in November 2023, the Indian government introduced the Drone Didi Scheme to empower women in rural areas.[7] Through this innovative scheme, rural women are provided with access to state-of-the-art drone technology and comprehensive training. Women, organized into self-help groups, are equipped with agricultural drones that enable them to actively participate in farming activities. From crop spraying to precision agriculture, field mapping and data collection, the scheme ensures that women play a significant role in agricultural innovation and development.

Overall, the integration of AI-driven drones in agriculture represents a paradigm shift in farming practices. By leveraging cutting-edge technology, farmers can overcome traditional challenges, enhance productivity and ensure sustainable agricultural practices for future generations. The initiatives taken by the Indian government underscore the transformative potential of drones not only in improving agricultural outcomes but also in promoting gender equality and rural empowerment.

Generative AI

In December 2022, Antony Aumann, a professor of philosophy at Northern Michigan University, acknowledged an essay as the best paper in the class in his course on world religions.[8] The essay discussed the morality of bans on the burqa (veil) using articulated language, convincing arguments and succinct examples. Upon enquiry, the student admitted to using ChatGPT, a chatbot that can create information, write articles, explain concepts and develop ideas in simple language.

Welcome to the world of generative AI. It refers to an AI system that can create new content, such as text, images or music, rather than simply analysing or acting on existing data. The generative AI model used for creating text, such as ChatGPT, relies on extensive training with large datasets to produce content resembling the input data. OpenAI introduced ChatGPT3 (Version 3.0) on 30 November 2022, and within a week it had garnered over one million users. By January 2024, the user base had expanded significantly to reach 180.5 million.[9] This variant of the GPT model is proficient at generating human-like text across various contexts and styles. ChatGPT can undergo fine-tuning for specific tasks like language translation, text summarization or question answering. It excels at open-ended tasks like conversations, that is, generating coherent responses by grasping the conversation's context. Additionally, it serves as a language model, providing accurate and natural language understanding and generation.

An example of a conversation with ChatGPT on two questions is reproduced in Box 5.0. The replies given by ChatGPT are indeed eye-opening. It is difficult to believe that such succinct and intelligent responses have been created by a machine.

> ### BOX 5.0: Conversation with ChatGPT (OpenAI) on 18 January 2023
>
> **How can artificial intelligence augment the capabilities of humans?**
>
> *Artificial intelligence (AI) can augment human capabilities in a variety of ways. Some examples include:*
>
> 1. ***Automating repetitive tasks:*** *AI can be used to automate repetitive and mundane tasks, freeing up human workers to focus on more complex and creative tasks.*
> 2. ***Enhancing decision-making:*** *AI can be used to analyse large amounts of data and provide insights that humans may not have been able to see on their own, which can help improve decision-making.*

3. **Assisting with physical tasks:** AI can be used to assist with physical tasks such as manufacturing, transportation and logistics, and construction.
4. **Improving communication:** AI-powered chatbots and virtual assistants can help improve communication and customer service.
5. **Enhancing human creativity:** AI can be used to generate new ideas and inspiration, which can help humans to be more creative.
6. **Identifying patterns and trends:** AI can be used to identify patterns and trends in data, which can help humans to make predictions and take action.
7. **Helping with medical diagnosis and treatment:** AI can be used to analyse medical images and assist with medical diagnosis and treatment.
8. **Assisting in research and scientific discovery.**
9. **Helping to create more human-like interaction with machines.**

AI is not a replacement of humans, but a tool to enhance human capabilities and productivity. It can help to boost efficiency and effectiveness in various fields and make humans' life easier.

 Will you replace humans?

 As an AI, my main purpose is to assist and augment human capabilities, not replace them. I am designed to perform tasks that are difficult or impossible for humans to do, such as analysing large amounts of data or automating repetitive processes. However, I do not have the ability to make decisions or to think creatively in the way that humans can.

AI is a tool, it can be used to improve human life and work, but it cannot replace the unique qualities of humans such as

> *creativity, emotions and decision-making.*
>
> *AI can be seen as a helper, rather than a replacement, for humans. It can help to boost efficiency and productivity, but humans will always be needed to provide oversight, to make decisions, and for their unique skills and abilities.*

The above replies are indicative of the potential of generative AI in creating contextual text. ChatGPT can also write essays, poems, letters, applications and résumés for given skill sets; summarize text; write, debug and explain software codes; solve mathematical problems with explanations; write stories for a given context; tell jokes; translate text; and much more. A tool like ChatGPT can save humans lots of effort. In the words of ChatGPT, 'As a language model, I can assist humans by providing them with information, answering questions, generating text and helping with language-related tasks. I can help with research, writing, language translation, and much more. However, my capabilities are limited to language processing and do not extend to physical tasks.' ChatGPT is often compared with Google, which has revolutionized web search, with the former now emerging as the next breakthrough. After all, if an AI model is able to not only search for relevant information but also collate it, summarize it and produce a report, why would a person make the effort to search relevant websites on Google and then collate information from multiple websites?

ChatGPT-4 was launched on 14 March 2023, with a significant improvement in its capabilities over earlier versions. OpenAI is already working on releasing ChatGPT-5 in 2025, which is likely to present numerous enhancements beyond its predecessor's capabilities. It boasts superior reasoning abilities, enhanced image comprehension and an increased capacity to handle large documents, making it a more effective and adaptable tool.

OpenAI chief executive officer (CEO) Sam Altman, in an interview at the Aspen Ideas Festival in June 2024, stated, 'I expect it to be a significant leap forward. A lot of the things that GPT-4 gets wrong, you know, can't do much in the way of reasoning, sometimes just sort of totally goes off the rails and makes a dumb mistake, like even a six-year-old would never make.'[10]

Regenerative AI and Copyright

In 2022, Kristina Kashtanova, a New York-based author, released an 18-page comic titled *Zarya of the Dawn*. The comic showcases a character named Zarya who awakens in an abandoned New York City without any recollection of her past after centuries have passed. Kashtanova employed a regenerative AI tool called Midjourney to craft the visual elements of the book. By providing written prompts, she guided the AI tool to generate images that depict a futuristic world.

The copyright for the comic was officially granted in September 2022. Following this, Kashtanova took to social media to announce that authors are now eligible for legal protection for works created with AI's assistance. The notion of copyright for a work generated with an AI tool ignited a heated debate on the ethical considerations surrounding the use of AI in literary and artistic endeavours. The US

Copyright Office partially cancelled the copyright granted to her, stating:

> We conclude that Ms. Kashtanova is the author of the Work's text as well as the selection, coordination, and arrangement of the Work's written and visual elements. That authorship is protected by copyright. However, as discussed below, the images in the Work that were generated by the Midjourney technology are not the product of human authorship. Because the current registration for the Work does not disclaim its Midjourney-generated content, we intend to cancel the original certificate issued to Ms. Kashtanova and issue a new one covering only the expressive material that she created.[11]

The question remains: to what extent can works created by AI tools be claimed to be a product of human creativity and rightfully seek copyright? Is it ethical to even claim such a copyright? The claimant may always assert that the work, although created by AI, has been guided and prompted by them. There is no straight answer to this question, but the fact remains that AI tools can assist human beings in almost any work.

Embracing AI to Augment Human Capabilities

An article titled 'The Best Leaders Can't Be Replaced by AI' succinctly highlighted the importance of embracing AI and retaining human qualities depending upon the type of work involved.[12] AI surpasses humans in processing power and unbiased decision-making, and many employees prefer

AI for strategy and feedback. However, research indicates that effective leadership is rooted in human qualities. Employees value the authenticity, empathy and wisdom that only human leaders provide. AI excels at data analysis and consistency but struggles with understanding human emotions and complex interpersonal dynamics. Leaders should embrace AI's strengths while enhancing their own human qualities to foster trust and motivation. The future of leadership lies in balancing AI efficiency with human-centred approaches. The authors of the article recommend using a matrix, as depicted in Figure 5.2, to determine when leaders should utilize AI and when they should rely on their human qualities. This matrix helps leaders assess situations based on the need for analytical versus interpersonal skills, guiding them to integrate AI for data-heavy tasks and apply human empathy and wisdom for tasks requiring EI and personal interaction.

Strategizing and decision-making demand significant involvement from human leaders augmented by AI's capabilities. Research and data analytics benefit from high AI use without much human involvement. Tasks focusing on individual and team development require a strong human presence with limited AI support. Conversely, repetitive and simple tasks can be efficiently handled with AI engagement without much human support. Leaders must appropriately balance human and AI involvement for each task based on the need for data-driven insights and EI. This balanced approach ensures optimal performance and fosters a supportive and effective work environment.

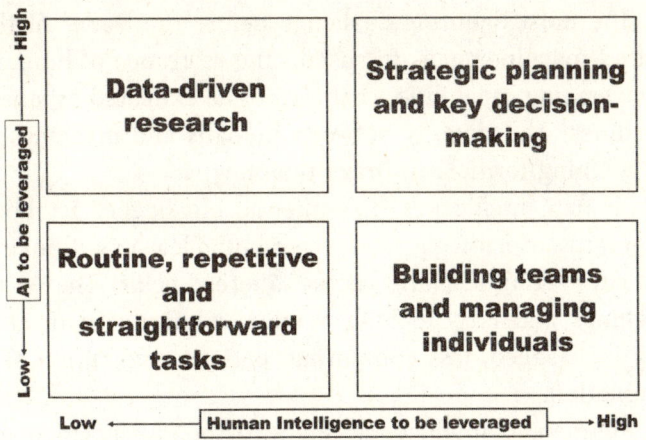

Figure 5.2[13]: Augmenting Human Qualities with AI

Challenges and Opportunities for Leaders of the VUCA World

How to use digital technologies to augment humans' capabilities and improve their productivity?

In the first machine age (Industry 1.0 to Industry 3.0), the competition was between the muscle power of humans and machines in which machines obviously prevailed. In the second machine age (Industry 4.0), the brain power of humans was challenged by machines. Humans can rule the animal world because of their cognitive abilities; however, this distinct characteristic is losing its uniqueness to machines. The examples discussed earlier in the chapter illustrate that humans need to appreciate the prowess of machines and work closely with them to improve their own efficiency.

The most daunting challenge before the leader of the second machine age is to sustain the relevance of humans by leveraging capabilities that cannot be emulated by smart machines. The synergy between humans and machines is the winning formula to brave this new world.

Human intelligence or authentic intelligence is about common sense, imagination, experiential learning, thinking and connecting learning across different fields. The AI of machines entails crunching a huge volume of data at a very high speed, fast computing, pattern recognition and automation.

Augmented intelligence refers to the enhancement of humans' cognitive abilities with the help of machines (Figure 5.3). The spellcheck feature of any word processor is the simplest example of the augmentation of humans' language skills with the help of machines. The use of Google Maps by vehicle drivers is another example of augmenting the navigational capabilities of human drivers using machines. Today, generative AI tools such as ChatGPT are emerging as game changers to assist humans with information, answering questions, generating text, and language-related tasks such as research and writing.

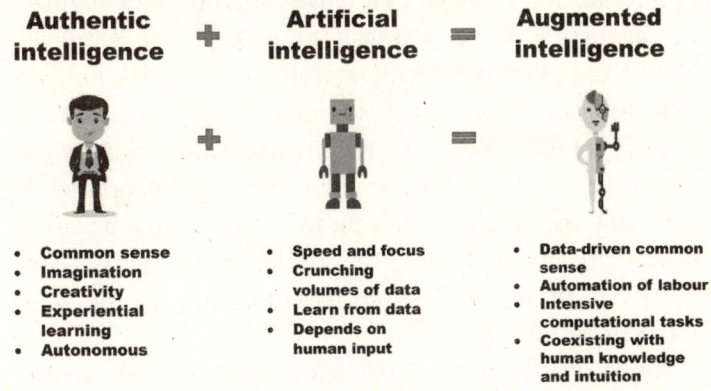

Figure 5.3: Augmented intelligence

Leaders need to reflect upon the following:

- Where and how machine intelligence can be synergized with humans to improve the productivity of the organization and reduce costs while retaining human qualities.
- How to augment the capabilities of human resources to make them more efficient and productive.

Leaders can enhance their skills and those of their teams by leveraging digital technologies to boost productivity. Regardless of business size, leaders can use AI tools to draft reports, compose letters, send emails, and more, all of which can increase efficiency and effectiveness. Enhancing employee productivity is one of the most effective ways to improve the bottom line. Applications such as employee self-service, project management tools, e-office, time management tools, asset tracking tools, internal communication tools and employee chatbots can augment the capabilities of employees. For example, an employee chatbot may assist them with salary-related queries, booking a meeting room, ordering stationary, applying for leave or even setting alerts and reminders, thus making these tasks very easy and less time-consuming. Generative AI tools such as ChatGPT can be used for writing a variety of content: emails, letters, reports and summarizing long text. After all, the time saved by employees is time saved by the organization.

Similarly, human qualities such as awareness, compassion and wisdom are essential in leadership because they foster trust, loyalty and motivation among employees. These traits enable leaders to understand and empathize with their team, navigate complex interpersonal dynamics and make decisions that consider the well-being of individuals. Authentic human interaction builds a supportive work environment, which encourages collaboration and innovation.

So the key to success is to augment the authentic intelligence of humans with the help of the AI of machines. If a leader is unable to leverage AI, the competitor will do it sooner rather than later and the leader will be left behind.

'Some people call this artificial intelligence, but the reality is this technology will enhance us. So instead of artificial intelligence, I think we'll augment our intelligence.'

—Ginni Rometty

6

Wary of Biases in Data

'We have to place our attention on humanizing artificial intelligence by removing the biases from algorithms rather than dehumanizing it.'

—Abhijit Naskar

AI AND ML MODELS FOR PREDICTIVE ANALYTICS ARE essentially trained and tested on volumes of data. The data can be labelled or unlabelled for supervised and unsupervised learning, respectively. Labelled data is data with a name tag. For example, in a set of images of dogs and cats, if we tag the images as a dog or a cat, the data becomes labelled data. The ML model trained on these data will be able to identify and tag new pictures of cats or dogs. This is called supervised learning because the data used to train the model is already labelled. Conversely, if the data used for training the ML model is not tagged and is raw (unsupervised), the model would cluster the data into two categories: animal A and animal B. Once a new image of a cat or a dog is processed in the model, it will identify the image as animal A or B. These are rudimentary examples of how ML uses the given data for training. The model, once developed, can be applied to a new set of data for analytics, prediction, forecasting recommendation and decision-making. The model's efficacy largely depends upon the veracity of the data used for training. The model will be as good, bad or biased as the data with which it has been trained. For example, if the model is trained using images of only black cats, it would only consider black cats as cats and misclassify white cats. In the absence of reliable data, the model would work on the principle of garbage in–garbage out. The challenges lie in identifying and segregating garbage data from authentic and trustworthy data. There have been a number of real-life cases when the use of biased data for training the model resulted in biased outcomes that impacted the lives of humans for whom such a model was intended.

Education Value-Added Assessment System

Daniel Santos was a social studies teacher at Navarro Middle School in Houston, which is managed by the Houston Independent School District (HISD) in Texas, US. Despite previously receiving awards for being an effective teacher, he was assessed as ineffective by the Education Value-Added Assessment System (EVAAS) in 2014.[1] The system adopted by HISD used a student's previous test scores to predict their academic growth for the current year but did not clearly define what was considered sufficient growth. EVAAS scores were used to assess performance and determine bonuses, promotions and disciplinary action for teachers. The system was developed by a private company, which did not share its algorithm with HISD and classified it as a trade secret.

In 2015, a group of teachers filed a lawsuit against the use of EVAAS, claiming that it used a flawed formula and did not consider factors such as a student's home life and other socio-economic factors that may affect their academic performance. The teachers argued that the system was proven to be unreliable and was also biased against teachers of specific subjects and a certain category of students.

The federal judge agreed with the teachers' main argument and allowed the lawsuit to continue until HISD settled the case. Audrey Amrein-Beardsley, who was serving as an expert witness on the case, reported that the EVAAS results were not only highly volatile on a year-to-year basis but were also biased against teachers of English Language Learners and highly mobile students. The number of students each teacher taught (i.e., class size) skewed teachers' value-added scores. The court concluded that HISD's value-added appraisal system posed a threat to the teachers' constitutionally protected property interests in employment. The court then went on to consider the argument that the use of EVAAS violated due process because it did not provide sufficient information for a teacher to meaningfully challenge terminations based on their EVAAS score. Finally, the HISD agreed to pay $237,000 in legal fees and stop using EVAAS to make personnel decisions as part of the settlement with the teachers.

The algorithm used to assess teachers' performance was found to be biased, using a flawed methodology, and termed a black box system in which the methodology is considered proprietary and confidential.

Correctional Offender Management Profiling for Alternative Sanctions

Correctional Offender Management Profiling for Alternative Sanctions (COMPAS) is a case management and decision support tool used by US courts to assess the likelihood of a defendant becoming a recidivist (a convicted criminal who reoffends, especially repeatedly).

In 2014, Brisha Borden was charged with burglary and theft of a bicycle.[2] Apparently, Brisha was getting late to pick up her sister from school when she found an unlocked bicycle and decided to ride it to school.

In a different but equally petty case, 41-year-old Vernon Prater was arrested for shoplifting goods worth $86.35 from a Home Depot store. Prater was an old offender, having been convicted of armed robberies in the past. He had already served a five-year term in prison.

However, when the two records were processed through COMPAS to predict the likelihood of each committing a future crime, Borden, who is black, was assessed as posing a high risk, whereas Prater, who is white, was assessed as being a low risk.

Two years later, Borden had not committed any new crimes, but Prater was again serving an eight-year prison term for stealing thousands of dollars' worth of electronics from a warehouse.

ProPublica, an independent nonprofit newsroom that conducts investigative journalism, investigated the use of COMPAS and reported the following[3]: 'The formula was particularly likely to falsely flag black defendants as future criminals, wrongly labelling them this way at almost twice the rate as white defendants. White defendants were mislabelled as low risk more often than black defendants.'

COMPAS was found to be biased against the black population because the data used for training the model had more cases of black offenders than white ones.

Amazon Hiring Software

Amazon uses an AI/ML-based algorithm to scan applications for hiring employees. In 2015, it was reported that the algorithm was biased against women.[4] When investigated, it was found that the model was trained based on the number of résumés submitted over the previous ten years, and because most of the applicants were men, it was trained to favour men over women.

AI Algorithm (Beauty.ai)

In 2016, an international beauty contest was judged by an AI algorithm called Beauty.ai. Aspirants from around the world submitted their photos to the algorithm. An algorithm free of human biases was expected to select the faces based on what constitutes real human beauty. However, to the embarrassment of the organizers, the algorithm selected the winners solely based on skin colour. When investigated, it was found that the algorithm was trained using hundreds of images from past beauty contests. According to Nisheeth K. Vishnoi, an associate professor at the School of Computer and Communication Sciences at Switzerland-based École Polytechnique Fédérale de Lausanne (EPFL), 'The algorithm made a fairly non-trivial correlation between skin colour and beauty. A classic example of bias creeping into an algorithm.'[5]

Bias in AI

AI bias refers to the biased outcomes generated by AI systems. These outcomes often mirror and perpetuate existing societal biases that encompass historical and contemporary inequalities. Bias in AI can be found in various ways, including the initial training data, the algorithm itself or the predictions produced by the system.

Unchecked bias in AI systems undermines the full potential of AI because distorted results foster mistrust among marginalized groups, such as people of colour, women and individuals with disabilities.

Identifying and addressing the sources of bias is crucial to mitigate its impact on AI systems. The following are some key areas where bias can originate:

- **Training Data Bias**

AI systems learn from patterns in data, so it is crucial to check the data for any signs of bias. This means looking at the groups represented in the data to ensure none are missing or have too much or too little representation. If there is bias, it could lead to problems like facial recognition systems that don't work well for some people or hiring tools that are unfair. Bias might also occur if the data are labelled inconsistently. Checking the data carefully can help ensure that AI tools work fairly for everyone.

- **Algorithmic Bias**

Flawed training data can lead to algorithms producing errors, generating unfair outcomes or amplifying existing biases. Programming errors, such as biased factor weighting, contribute to algorithmic bias and may unintentionally discriminate against certain demographics.

- **Cognitive Bias**

Individuals naturally introduce biases when processing information, which influence their judgement and decision-making. Cognitive biases may be introduced in AI systems through biased data selection or weighting; this leads to AI favouring certain demographics over others.

Effectively addressing AI bias requires a comprehensive examination of datasets, ML algorithms and system components. By identifying and rectifying the sources of bias, there is an opportunity to enhance the fairness and reliability of AI systems, hence fostering inclusivity and trust among diverse user groups.

Assessment and Remediation of Bias

Statistical tools are available to assess the biases of the ML model. One of the most used tests for biases is the statistical parity test. The goal of this test is to determine the probability of achieving a favourable outcome for different groups. An equal probability indicates an unbiased model. A classic example is the ML model used for recruitment purposes. It should ensure that male and female candidates have an equal opportunity of being hired. If the model is biased, the result would show that one group is preferred over the other group, that is, the probability of hiring one group is more than that of another group.

Once the model is found to be biased, the next challenge is to remove the biases from the data. There can be broadly five types of biases in the ML models[6]:

- Sample bias is when the data collected are not representative of the population. For example, if the collected data have 80 per cent inputs from men when there are 60 per cent men in your organization. This bias can be controlled by selecting random data from a representative sample in proportion to the share of each segment of the actual population.
- Exclusion bias is when some features are excluded from the dataset during data cleaning under the assumption that some features are not important. A thorough analysis of the factors impacting the outcome of the model can help address exclusion biases.
- Observer bias is the tendency to see what we expect or what we want to see. A data scientist's biased views may creep into the model itself. These biases can be controlled by selecting a team of data scientists from diverse backgrounds, training them on the possibility of biases and having well-defined rules and procedures for experimentation.
- Prejudice bias is the result of cultural influences or stereotypical inputs in the data. For example, if the data show that most women are housewives and men are officegoers, the ML model trained on this data

will predict that every woman is a housewife. These biases can be identified using the statistical parity test and can be reduced by ignoring the statistical relationship between gender and occupation or any other characteristic that should not affect the result.
- Measurement bias occurs when the device used for measuring data has some issue. For example, if a thermometer used to measure temperature is not suitable for measuring sub-zero temperature, the data for the sub-zero range will not be reliable. These kinds of biases can be reduced by using multiple devices for measurement and periodically checking the data collected by well-trained professionals.

Challenges and Opportunities for Leaders of the VUCA World

How to detect biases and remove biases from the data used by my organization?

From the above examples it is evident that developing an unbiased algorithm is easier said than done. Many times, it is not even known that the algorithm is biased. The challenge before the leaders of the VUCA world is to be cautious of the biases in the algorithm used by their organization. For instance, whether it is favouring or disfavouring a class of customers if it is used for demand prediction, whether it is biased against any race/class/gender if it is used for assessing the performance of employees, and so on. Data scientists aiming to develop an unbiased algorithm need to ensure that the data used for training the model are free of any bias. Sometimes, the biases of the data scientist may also inadvertently creep into the model. The model trained and developed using a given set of data may be tested on different social groups, whether that be by gender, ethnicity or age, and any biases, if found, be addressed. A leader has to ensure that bias-free data are used for ML and that the results are thoroughly validated before deploying the model.

The leaders will have to use their own innovative ways to find biases in the data and eliminate them to ensure that the ML model trained using these data is free from any bias and is reliable. This job cannot be left to the data scientist team as they may be unaware of their own biases or biases in data.

Challenges and opportunities walk hand in hand. An unbiased model may be a competitive advantage for an organization. Leaders may boast about the fairness of the algorithms they use as their unique selling point (USP) and competitive advantage over their competitors.

'I think unconscious bias is one of the hardest things to get at.'

—Ruth Bader Ginsburg

7

Process Innovation

'Electricity is an example of a general purpose technology, like the steam engine before it. General purpose technologies drive most economic growth because they unleash cascades of complementary innovations, like lightbulbs and, yes, factory redesign.'

—Erik Brynjolfsson

BORN IN NEWINGTON, SURREY, ENGLAND, ON 22 SEPTEMBER 1791, he had only an elementary education.[1] At the tender age of 14 years, he started working as a bookbinder for a bookseller in London. He had a deep interest in the sciences, too. As a bookbinder, he got the opportunity to read the many books that he would receive for binding. During the day, he would bind the books, and during the night, he would read. Through these readings, he developed a keen interest in electricity. He was particularly inspired by the book *Conversations on Chemistry* by Jane Marcet. In 1812, at the age of 20 years, he got an opportunity to attend lectures by the most eminent chemist of the time: Humphry Davy. He attended all his lectures with great earnestness and prepared detailed notes. Later, he sent those notes to Davy with a request to work for the latter. Davy was impressed by the notes and employed him as a chemical assistant at the Royal Institution on 1 March 1813. In 1813–15, he accompanied Davy as a scientific attendant and valet on a long tour of the continent. Although he was not treated well by Davy's wife during the trip, it provided him with access to Europe's scientific elite.

Soon, he established himself as an experimenter who showed keen interest in experimenting with innovative ideas, even inventing and making new equipment to test these ideas. Although he worked mostly in chemistry, his life-changing invention was that of the electric motor. Through his experiments, he proved the existence of a relationship between magnetism and electricity. In 1821, he discovered that when a magnet is moved inside the coil of a copper wire, a tiny electric current is generated through the wire. Later, this discovery became the foundation of the invention of electric motors. In 1831, he published his theory of induction, which predicts how a magnetic field interacts with an electric circuit to produce an electromotive force. He was the first to generate an electric current from a magnetic field and invented the first electric motor and dynamo. Many readers would have guessed by now whom we are talking about. Yes, he was Michael Faraday.

Michael Faraday (1791–1867)[2]

Till 1800, electricity was only considered a static charge that was used by magicians for the purpose of entertainment. Machines producing static electricity were for fun and were nicknamed parlour trick machines. In 1800, the first battery (voltaic pile) as a continuous source of electricity had been invented by Italian physicist Alessandro Volta. Though the concept of electricity was known for years, its real potential could only be harnessed with Michael Faraday's groundbreaking research in the field of electromagnetism.

Soon, there was unprecedented growth in inventions based on the use of electricity. The pace of invention was electrified in the true sense. In 1831, Joseph Henry developed a prototype direct current (DC) motor. In 1836, Nicholas Callan invented the transformer. In 1844, Samuel Morse developed telegraphy and the Morse code. In 1856, Charles Bourseul proposed telephony. In 1876, Alexander Graham Bell invented the telephone. In 1877, Thomas Alva Edison invented the phonograph. In 1878, Joseph Swan invented the incandescent light bulb. In 1879, Edison introduced a long-lasting filament for the incandescent lamp. In 1887, Nikola Tesla invented the first induction motor.

The First Industrial Revolution (1760–1870) in the late eighteenth century was led by the mechanization of manufacturing and production processes using steam power. The driving force for the Second Industrial Revolution (1870–1970) was electricity. Once it was possible to generate, transmit and store electricity, scientists started finding ways to use it to power anything and everything. Electricity was the major source of process innovation across industries. The processes that were mechanized during the First Industrial Revolution were progressively electrified to improve productivity and efficiency. Electricity formed the bedrock for process innovation during the Second Industrial Revolution. Electricity also paved the way for product innovation, such as the invention of light bulbs, electric cars, electric locomotives, radios, refrigerators, TVs, mixers, washing machines and motorbikes.

The Third Industrial Revolution (1970–2000), led by automation and computerization, reaped the benefits of the First and Second Industrial Revolutions.

Computerization helped streamline industrial processes to improve productivity and reduce costs. The automation of manufacturing further reduced costs and improved quality as well as productivity. Software development emerged as a sunrise sector with unlimited possibilities. Like electricity, computerization and automation were used for process innovation across industries. Today, it is difficult to fathom an industry without computerization. Computers have become the building blocks for all sectors of the economy.

The Fourth Industrial Revolution since 2000 is building upon the Third Industrial Revolution. It is characterized by a fusion of technologies that is blurring the lines among the physical, digital and biological spheres. The building blocks for this phase of the Industrial Revolution include AI/ML, robotics, IoT, 3D printing, genetic engineering, quantum computing, and other technologies.

Process Innovation in the Fourth Industrial Revolution

AI is often called new electricity. AI's comparison to the invention of electricity is apt due to its transformative impact on society. Just as electricity revolutionized countless industries from manufacturing to communication, AI is reshaping our world. Its applications span from healthcare and finance to transportation and entertainment, enhancing efficiency and innovation. Like electricity, AI has become foundational, powering technologies like ML and automation. Its potential for positive change is immense, promising to solve complex problems and improve human lives. As electricity illuminated the world, AI illuminates our future, driving progress and innovation in previously unimaginable ways. AI is already leading process innovation across all sectors of the economy.

> *'Just as electricity transformed almost everything 100 years ago, today I actually have a hard time thinking of an industry that I don't think AI will transform in the next several years.'*
>
> —Andrew Ng

Although innovation has always been crucial to an organization's long-term success, in this AI era, further innovation is required to exploit the potential of AI/ML to improve productivity, engage customers and employees, improve service delivery, and optimize business processes. During the industrial era, leaders were focused on product innovation and differentiation as a means of staying competitive and meeting the evolving needs of their customers. By adding new features and differentiating their products, companies were able to gain a competitive advantage in crowded markets, which helped fuel the growth of industry and commerce during this era. Mobile companies launching new mobile phone models with additional features almost every year is an example of a product differentiation strategy to woo customers to buy new mobile phones. However, in the Fourth Industrial Revolution, data-driven production creates vast opportunities for process innovation to not only bring efficiency but also to be more responsive and agile to serve customers better. Just as electricity was used to transform processes in the early twentieth century to improve productivity and efficiency, AI/ML solutions are being deployed for process innovation.

Some examples of process innovations fuelled by AI/ML already taking place in the AI era are presented below.

Manufacturing

Robots have been used in factories since the 1960s. In 2000, the era of smart robotics started, which marked the onset of the fourth generation of robots characterized by enhanced intelligence. These advanced robots use sophisticated computer programs that are capable of learning. Equipped with refined sensors, these machines enable controllers to efficiently adapt to diverse circumstances. Recent developments in AI, speech recognition, computer vision and neural networks have paved the way for truly intelligent robots that can take verbal commands, recognize things, think, understand and work like human beings to some extent. Amazon uses an army of robots in its huge fulfilment centres (warehouses) to bring products to humans who package them for further dispatch to the end customer. The process innovation in fulfilment centres is driving Amazon's one-day delivery programme.

In addition to the advancements in smart robotics, the concept of a smart shop floor has also gained prominence in recent years. The adoption of digital tools in manufacturing, which constitutes the smart shop floor under Industry 4.0, has transformed production processes. This includes IoT devices, sensors and analytics to create a networked ecosystem for real-time monitoring and optimization. Connected systems enhance agility, that is, adjustments based on dynamic factors. The synergy of smart robotics and the smart shop floor improves manufacturing efficiency, offering a flexible production environment. Companies like Amazon benefit from increased productivity, cost reduction and improved customer satisfaction through rapid and accurate order processing. Ongoing smart technology integration on the shop floor continues to drive innovation and efficiency in manufacturing.

In an article titled 'How India Inc Is Boosting Productivity by Using Intelligent Technologies', *The Economic Times* reported that 'Assembly lines are becoming less dependent on humans—the shop floor foreman's holler is headed toward extinction. Instead, data and intelligent technologies have taken charge of factory machines, instructing them on tasks that need to be completed.'[3]

Health

AI is able to analyse huge amounts of data stored by hospitals in the form of doctors' prescriptions, medical test reports and images. AI can identify patterns and insights often undetectable by manual human skill sets. AI is already being deployed to detect diseases, such as cancer, more accurately and in their early stages. The collection of data through wearables and other medical devices and subsequent analytics through AI tools is also being used to detect early-stage heart disease, enabling healthcare professionals to better monitor and detect potentially life-threatening episodes at earlier, more treatable stages. Process innovation in the early detection of diseases, real-time monitoring and disease management through AI has transformed the health sector.

Further, AI uses genetic data to predict diseases

by analysing DNA sequences to identify patterns and correlations that indicate disease risk. ML algorithms, including supervised and unsupervised learning, help uncover associations between genetic variations and diseases. Polygenic risk scores and genome-wide association studies are tools used to assess risk for conditions like cancer, cardiovascular diseases, neurological disorders and metabolic diseases. This approach facilitates personalized medicine, tailored treatments and early intervention.

Transportation

The First Industrial Revolution was driven by steam-powered engines that transformed transportation. Today, AI/ML is emerging as the new engine of growth in the transportation industry. There have been significant advancements in the use of AI, ML, deep learning and IoT to innovate traditional processes to improve the efficiency, safety and sustainability of transportation systems.

One key area of focus for AI/ML in transportation is the development of self-driving vehicles. These vehicles use sensors and cameras to navigate roads and make real-time decisions with the ultimate goal of reducing accidents and fatalities and increasing the efficiency of transportation networks.

In addition to self-driving vehicles, AI/ML is also being used for transport demand prediction, which can help transportation planners and operators anticipate and respond to changes in demand for different modes of transportation. This can improve the efficiency and reliability of transportation networks, leading to reduced travel times and improved customer satisfaction.

Another important application of AI/ML in transportation is traffic congestion management. AI/ML can analyse traffic data and identify patterns and trends, which can then be used to optimize traffic flow and reduce congestion on roads and highways.

AI/ML is also used for traffic detection, pedestrian detection and traffic flow analysis, allowing for the real-time monitoring and management of transportation networks. Computer vision-powered parking management, automated licence plate recognition and automatic traffic incident detection are other applications of AI/ML in transportation, all of which can improve efficiency and safety in the transportation sector.

AI/ML is also being used in the predictive maintenance of assets to replace manual processes with automated ones. By using data analytics and ML algorithms, transportation operators can identify potential maintenance issues before they become major problems, thus reducing downtime and improving asset utilization.

For instance, the Delhi Metro Rail Corporation (DMRC) has replaced traditional manual inspection methods with an advanced AI-driven system called TrackVue to enhance track inspection and maintenance processes. This innovative system employs high-resolution cameras, lasers and inertial sensors mounted on a train to scan the rails when the train is moving. By doing so, it effectively evaluates track conditions, identifies potential issues like damaged or worn components and records critical rail–wheel interactions to detect damages. It allows for the early detection of defects, cracks and foreign objects to ensure that proactive measures can be taken to uphold passenger and staff safety. Moreover, TrackVue facilitates better maintenance planning by providing comprehensive data and analytics. This empowers DMRC to develop precise maintenance schedules and prioritize repairs based on the severity of defects, thus optimizing maintenance efforts and minimizing downtime for repairs.

Overall, the use of AI/ML in transportation is transforming the sector in numerous important ways, leading to increased efficiency, safety and sustainability. As the Fourth Industrial Revolution continues to evolve, we can expect to see even more advancements in the use of AI/ML in transportation, ultimately leading to more seamless and efficient transportation systems.

Supply Chain/Network: The Control Tower Approach

The modern supply chain is a complex network that connects various entities, including manufacturers, suppliers, distributors, retailers and customers. Traditionally, this supply chain operated linearly, with goods flowing from one stage to the next. However, in recent times, there has been a significant shift towards an interconnected and dynamic system that has transformed the supply chain into a supply network.

This evolution is driven by the integration of digital technologies such as IoT, big data, AI, blockchain and robotics. These technologies are deployed to revolutionize traditional business processes and elevate efficiency within the supply chain. One notable transformation is the emergence of a 'control tower' concept in supply chain management. Unlike the linear approach, the control tower envisions a centralized hub that provides real-time visibility into every aspect of the supply chain, both internally and externally. This means that stakeholders throughout the supply chain are digitally connected, facilitating seamless communication and collaboration.

The control tower approach involves integrating all components of the supply chain, including suppliers, manufacturers, distributors and logistics providers, on a unified digital platform. This integration fosters greater collaboration, coordination and efficiency across the entire supply chain. The use of advanced analytics and ML algorithms further enhances this approach by providing a comprehensive and dynamic view of the supply chain.

One of the key advantages of the control tower is its ability to offer a quick response to potential disruptions or delays. By capturing and utilizing near-real-time operational data from across the business ecosystem, the control tower enhances decision-making processes. This real-time visibility allows companies to identify issues as they arise and respond promptly, thereby mitigating the impact of disruptions on the supply chain.

Thus, adopting a control tower approach provides companies with a more complete and accurate understanding of their supply chain operations. This leads to improved overall performance, increased operational efficiency and higher levels of customer satisfaction. Gartner defines a supply chain control tower as a concept that results in combining people, processes, data, organization and technology.[4]

Challenges and Opportunities for Leaders of the VUCA World

How to innovate business processes to be more responsive and agile to customers' needs?

In today's VUCA world, organizations must strive to digitalize their business processes to stay competitive. Leaders need to take a deep dive into their current processes and identify opportunities for digitalization to innovate and streamline these processes. They need to identify areas where they can introduce digitalization to enhance processes and ultimately gain a competitive advantage over their rivals. The digitalization of processes is not only about internal operations but also about integration with customers, suppliers and other stakeholders to meet their needs.

Customers today expect real-time information, quick and personalized services and interaction through digital means. Digital integration with stakeholders is fundamental to meeting these expectations. For instance, suppliers need to be integrated into the IT platform of an organization to facilitate the real-time sharing of data, predictive analytics and demand forecasting. In turn, this digital integration with suppliers enables organizations to be more responsive to customers' needs.

Digitalizing business processes goes beyond enhancing operational efficiency; it's also about elevating the customer experience. Digitalization enables organizations to offer real-time information, personalized services and quicker response times. It also enables them to predict and respond to customer needs efficiently.

Moreover, digitalization can help organizations identify new business opportunities by analysing data generated from various sources, such as social media, weather, competitors, stakeholders and the government. These data, both structured and unstructured, can be used for analysis, prediction and gaining deep insights into the business. By leveraging these data, organizations can improve business performance in terms of productivity, profitability, efficiency, and customer and employee satisfaction, and much more.

Conclusively, leaders must challenge themselves to identify opportunities for digitalization in their business processes. Digitalization is fundamental to meeting customer needs and staying competitive. By innovating their processes, leveraging data and adopting a well-thought-out digital change management plan, organizations can transform their operations and improve their bottom line. The VUCA world requires leaders to embrace digitalization as an opportunity rather than see it as a threat and to focus on innovation to stay ahead of the competition.

The next chapter is devoted to the change leader.

> *'Innovation distinguishes between
> a leader and a follower.'*
>
> —Steve Jobs

8

Change Leader: Agile and Adaptable

> *'According to Darwin's* Origin of Species, *it is not the most intellectual of the species that survives; it is not the strongest that survives; but the species that survives is the one that is able best to adapt and adjust to the changing environment in which it finds itself.'*
>
> —Leon C. Megginson

GEORGE EASTMAN, THE FOUNDER OF THE FAMOUS KODAK company, was born on 12 July 1854 in a village near New York. His father died at a young age, leaving behind George, his mother and two sisters, one of whom was disabled due to polio. He had to quit school at the age of 14 and start working as an office boy at an insurance company and later as a clerk at a local bank.

At the age of 24, he planned a vacation to Santo Domingo and decided to carry a camera along with him. The cameras in those days were as big as microwave ovens and required a heavy tripod, glass plates, chemicals, glass tank, water, etc. Before taking the photograph, emulsion had to be applied on the glass plates; then, these wet plates were exposed to light to capture the image. The exposed plates had to be developed before they dried up. The complete outfit 'was a pack-horse load', as he described it.[1] Although he could not go on vacation, he was convinced that the process of photography needed to be simplified to make it available to the masses.

He started working on finding some solution to make plates that retained sensitivity after they were dry and could be exposed when required. These so-called dry plates would not have required the application of the emulsion solution just before taking the photograph. During the day he worked in the bank, and at night he experimented in his mother's kitchen. His devotion and hard work paid off by 1880 when he invented a workable formula for creating dry plates and got the machine patented for preparing large numbers of such plates.

On 1 January 1881, the Eastman Dry Plate Company was founded. The company has been called Eastman Kodak Company since 1892. Eastman continued his quest to find an alternative to the glass plates. He was looking for a convenient, flexible and lighter material that could easily be carried around for photography. He started by coating the photographic emulsion on paper, called film, and then loading the paper on to a roll holder.

In 1888, Eastman introduced the KODAK camera, thus beginning an era of photography. It was a simple box camera, easy to handle, preloaded with a 100-exposure roll of film and priced at $25. Once the roll was finished, the entire camera had to be sent to a factory where it was reloaded with another film. The camera was returned to the customer, and the exposed roll was processed to develop photographs, all for $10.

The simplification of camera technology and film processing in factories democratized photography, making it accessible to millions of amateurs without them needing professional training or expertise. Eastman introduced a highly effective marketing campaign that showcased women and children conveniently using the camera and coined a memorable slogan: 'You press the button, we do the rest.'

During the twentieth century, Kodak continued to gain popularity and profits soared. For decades, Kodak remained the market leader in producing photographic material. In the 1970s, Kodak's global market share in the field of photography was around 80 per cent. Kodak followed the 'razor and blades' business model, which entails selling razors at a small profit margin and blades (consumables) at a higher profit margin. Kodak sold cameras at an affordable price with a small profit margin and consumables such as films, printing sheets and other accessories at a high profit margin. Kodak was generating significantly more revenue from the sale of films and printing of pictures than from the sale of cameras.

While the world was undergoing a transformation with the start of the Third Industrial Revolution in the 1970s, computerization and digitalization, Kodak's management was too busy minting money from its films and printing. In 1973, Steven Sasson, a 23-year-old electrical engineer, started working for Eastman Kodak. He was assigned seemingly unimportant work: to explore any practical use of the charged coupled devices (CCDs) that had been invented a few years back. These have light-sensitive sensors that can convert light into electrical signals. Using CCDs, Sasson could capture the image, convert it into digital form and store the final image on a digital magnetic tape. The picture could then be seen on a TV set. By 1974, he was ready with his life-changing invention: the first digital camera. When Sasson presented his invention to Kodak's management, he was told, 'That's cute, but don't tell anyone about it. That's how you shoot yourself in the foot!'[2] Excessively fixated on the profitability of the film and printing industry, Kodak's leadership ignored the rise of digital cameras. The corporate giant, akin to a dinosaur, seemed too colossal to recognize the impending threat posed by digitalization. The management at Kodak staunchly believed that individuals cherished the tangible experience of holding physical photos on paper. They thought that no one would ever want to look at their pictures on a TV set. Personal computers were still fancy and could have been used to view digital images. Although the first digital camera, called the electronic still camera (ecam), was patented in 1978, Sasson was strictly advised to refrain from talking about it in public. While Kodak kept the idea of digital cameras a secret, other competitors started working on digital cameras. By the time Kodak realized what customers wanted—digital images that could be stored and shared online—competitors had already gained an edge. In 2004, Kodak announced it would stop the sale of traditional cameras. Finally, having failed to compete in the digital camera market, Kodak filed for bankruptcy in 2012. The so-called 'Google of the 1950s' failed to keep pace with the rapid digitalization that was creeping into every sphere of human life following the principle of Moore's law.[*]

---

[*]Moore's law is the principle that the speed and capability of computers can be expected to double every two years as a result of increases in the number of transistors a microchip can contain.

Blockbuster Busted by Netflix

In 1997, Reed Hastings, a software developer, had to pay a late fee of $40 to Blockbuster when he forgot to return a rented video cassette of the movie *Apollo 13*. At the time, Blockbuster was the biggest video rental company in the US. Its first store opened in Dallas, Texas, in 1985, and over the next 20 years, it rose to become the leading movie rental business in the country. In those days, people could watch movies that were not running in theatres from the comfort of their homes by renting video cassettes from rental stores like Blockbuster. Another option was to buy these cassettes, which was costlier and the cassette was of no use once watched. Hence, Blockbuster was a big success. In just five years (by 1990), Blockbuster had opened over 1,000 stores in the US.[3] The customer used to visit the Blockbuster store, select the video cassette to watch on weekends and pay the rent. They were required to pay a late fee if the video cassettes were returned later than the mentioned date. It is said that 16 per cent of their annual revenue (around $800 million) was generated from late fee in the mid-1990s. Late fee had been the norm in the rental business to motivate customers to return video cassettes in time because business depended on how many times a tape could be rented in its useful life. However, the late fee was a persistent cause of annoyance to customers. Hastings' frustration at having to pay the $40 late fee was palpable. He immediately saw an opportunity to disrupt the movie-renting business. In 1997, Hastings and one of his co-workers, Marc Randolph, founded Netflix with 'no late fee' as one of its USPs. In 1998, Netflix started renting digital video discs (DVDs) when Blockbuster was renting video cassettes. Customers could select the DVDs online, which were sent to the customers via post, thus saving on the cost of brick-and-mortar stores. At that time, DVD players were expensive and possessed by a few, but Netflix founders could read the writing on the wall—DVDs were coming sooner than expected. Netflix joined hands with Toshiba, HP and Sony and offered free DVD rentals to new DVD player buyers.[4] When Blockbuster was charging per video cassette, Netflix started a monthly subscription model that allowed customers to order unlimited DVDs for a fixed fee per month and, most notably, with no late fee. Netflix introduced its online streaming service in January 2007. Initially, it offered a selection of movies and TV shows for streaming over the internet, allowing subscribers to watch content instantly on their computers. This marked a significant shift away from the traditional DVD-by-mail model that Netflix had started with.

During the initial years, Blockbuster was Netflix's biggest competitor. Realizing the potential for synergy between the two companies, Hastings and Randolph offered to sell their company to Blockbuster for $50 million, but the latter simply laughed at this proposal, turning a blind eye to the rapid evolution of online business. They kept opening more retail stores, having 9,000 stores and 60,000 employees across the globe by 2004. Facing stiff competition from Netflix, Blockbuster started online services, but it was too late to catch up with the headway made by Netflix. Blockbuster also withdrew the late fee, but again, this was too late to make much of a dent in improving its market share in the movie rental business. Blockbuster could not offload the burden of its inefficient DVD rental business and could not adapt to customers' changing needs. By 2007, Netflix had realized that DVD rental would not be profitable for long and chose to focus on its online streaming service because increasing number of people were accessing the internet at their homes. It realized that customers did not want DVDs but the convenience of ordering movies from their couches without any hassle of returning the DVDs. Netflix envisioned this shift and used its IT advantage to offer customers digital content with personalized services at a very affordable cost, which traditional retail stores could never have matched.

Netflix's recommendation system is one of its key features that sets it apart from other streaming services. The platform uses ML algorithms to analyse a user's viewing history and preferences and then recommends titles that are likely to be of interest to them. This personalized marketing approach not only improves user experience but also helps Netflix retain subscribers and increase engagement on the platform.

In 2010, Blockbuster filed for bankruptcy. Blockbuster's market leadership was busted by Netflix in just seven years, and the rest is history.

Nokia

The story of Nokia's fall is not very different from the above two examples. The Finnish giant was the largest mobile phone maker in 1998. Almost everyone owned a Nokia mobile phone before the days of the smartphone. In early 2007, Nokia was a dominant player in the mobile phone market, boasting a market share of more than 50 per cent. However, over the next five years, Nokia's presence in the mobile phone market declined dramatically, with its market share dwindling to almost zero by the end of 2012. Nokia failed to adapt to the smartphone revolution driven by the Android operating system. If Nokia's leadership had monitored the evolving technological trends and embraced smartphone technology, the company might have maintained its position as a leader in the mobile phone industry. They should have paid closer attention to developments in mobile technology, competitor strategies, customer preferences and the emerging opportunities resulting from the convergence of various technologies like mobile, music, cameras, gaming and videos.

From 1955 to 2017, 90 per cent of the Fortune 500 companies have fallen mostly due to a lack of adaptability to disruptive digital technologies.

Challenges and Opportunities for Leaders of the VUCA World

How is the ecosystem changing? How to adapt and remain ahead?

One common thread connecting the fall of behemoths discussed above is the lack of adaptability to the changing business environment. The pace of technological advancement corresponds to the speed of light in the virtual world of data, and product life is getting shorter day by day. The average smartphone's life is 12–24 months. Leaders need to adapt to this pace of change and use technology to keep their organizations ahead. They also have to keep themselves abreast with the upcoming technologies. Knowing technology is necessary but not sufficient as we have seen in the case of the invention of the digital camera by Kodak engineers. They should be able to visualize ways of adopting new technologies to improve their businesses. The writing on the wall may not be very clear, but leaders must understand it and act on it. Just like dinosaurs, the leaders of the VUCA world face an unprecedented risk of becoming fossils if they are unable to adapt to the rapid changes and keep pace with digital transformation.

Greek philosopher Heraclitus of Ephesus said, 'The only constant in life is change.' Unlike any other change, the digitalization of business processes is happening rather more quickly. The reality of today is that change is constant and swift. The pace of change due to digitalization makes change management challenging. Employees may perceive digitalization as a threat to their jobs. It is advisable to introduce digitalization from the top and set examples. Clear communication with employees to address their apprehensions is important to instil in them a trust in the process. The disruption caused by the adoption of digital technologies needs to be minimized by phased roll-outs and training employees to adapt to the changes. The benefits of process digitalization for employees may be discussed openly and transparently.

There are numerous opportunities to leverage digitalization, embrace change, and implement effective change management. Rapid adaptability can become a competitive advantage, boosting productivity and efficiency, meeting customer expectations, and ultimately outpacing competitors.

'Without change there is no innovation, creativity, or incentive for improvement. Those who initiate change will have a better opportunity to manage the change that is inevitable.'

—William Pollard

9

Coopetition: An Ecosystem Approach

'Competition has been shown to be useful up to a certain point and no further, but cooperation, which is the thing we must strive for today, begins where competition leaves off.'

—Franklin D. Roosevelt

Coopetition

Coopetition is the new buzzword in the lexicon of businesses in the AI era. It refers to the collaboration between companies that are also competitors. When businesses engage in competition and cooperation, they are practising coopetition. Using a strategic blend of cooperation with suppliers, customers and firms that produce complementary or related products, certain businesses can gain an advantage. Many IT platforms are promoting coopetition among businesses by offering options to integrate and exchange data. Some examples of coopetition are as follows:

Code Sharing in the Airlines Industry

Code sharing among airlines is a thriving example of coopetition and perhaps the earliest one. The history of code sharing can be traced back to the 1960s.[1] Code sharing in the airlines industry is when two or more airlines agree to sell tickets for the same flight under their own airline code while one of these airlines operates the flight.

For example, Airline A may operate a flight, but it also allows Airline B to sell tickets for that flight under Airline B's flight number. This allows both airlines to expand their reach by offering more flights and destinations to their customers without having to operate all the flights themselves.

Code sharing also allows airlines to form partnerships and alliances with other airlines, which can result in benefits to customers, such as smoother connections, easier baggage transfers and access to lounges and other airport facilities.

Code-sharing agreements facilitate airlines to offer frequent and abundant flights without any additional equipment, resources or costs. The code-sharing arrangement helps participating (and competing) airlines to enhance their revenue through cooperation and by offering the desired level of services to passengers. Code sharing offers more connections. Passengers are also able to fly on different airlines with a single ticket and are protected if any delays arise.

Overall, code sharing can benefit both airlines (Airline A and Airline B) and passengers by increasing the number of flights and destinations available to passengers, improving connections and convenience for them, and promoting greater cooperation and competition within the airlines industry.

Infrastructure Sharing by Telecom Companies

The telecom industry worldwide follows a strategy of sharing infrastructure to keep investments low and to compete for economies of scale. For example, a mobile tower set up by one telecom company can be offered on rent to other telecom companies for installing their telecom equipment. This kind of arrangement not only optimizes the return on investment in installing the tower but is also a necessity as the space available in cities for the installation of towers is limited. Such coopetition among participating companies is a win–win for all irrespective of competitive rivalries among them.

Development of Vaccines for COVID-19

In March 2020, Pfizer, an American multinational pharmaceutical and biotechnology corporation, and BioNTech, a German biotechnology company, entered into an agreement to jointly develop a vaccine for COVID-19. Pfizer and BioNTech are dominant competitors in the pharmaceutical market. The agreement facilitated both companies to synergize their research, development, testing and manufacturing capabilities. The coopetition enabled them to get the vaccine to the market by the end of 2020 and helped them produce hundreds of millions of doses in 2021.

Coopetition in Agriculture

365FarmNet is a digital platform in Europe that serves as an IT hub connecting various stakeholders in the agricultural sector.[2] This platform fosters collaboration among farm equipment manufacturers, financial institutions, chemical companies, seed producers, agricultural advisory services and even government agencies, such as the European Global Navigation Satellite Systems (GNSS) Agency. One of the key features of this platform is the development of a digital ecosystem where participants, including competitors, come together to share and utilize data. This cooperative and competitive approach allows these diverse stakeholders to benefit from each other's resources, expertise and information without compromising their individual interests.

The digital ecosystem facilitates the exchange of data related to various aspects of agriculture, including geolocation, diagnostics, crops, fertilizers and weather conditions. These shared data are made accessible to farmers through convenient channels such as smartphones or direct connections with farm equipment. By providing easy access to data and analysis, farmers can make informed decisions to optimize their agricultural practices, improve yields and enhance overall efficiency.

This coopetition model is beneficial for all participants in the ecosystem. For farm equipment makers, it opens up opportunities to integrate their products with valuable data and services. Financial institutions like Allianz can leverage data insights for risk assessment and to tailor insurance products for farmers. Chemical companies like Bayer can contribute knowledge on crop protection and enhance the effectiveness of agricultural practices. Seed producers like KWS Saat can use data to improve breeding and seed development. Agricultural advisory services by companies like Agravis can offer informed recommendations based on comprehensive data analysis. The European GNSS Agency contributes to location-based services, further enhancing the precision and efficiency of farming operations.

Apple and Samsung

Apple uses the Super Retina and Super Retina XDR displays, which use organic light-emitting diode (OLED) technology for the iPhone X series and later models. These screens are procured from Samsung, Apple's arch-competitor in the mobile phone market.[3] Samsung could have decided not to supply OLED screens to Apple so that the iPhone could not have competed with Samsung in the high-end smartphone market. However, Samsung is not the only supplier of OLED screens. Apple could have bought them from other producers like LG. Furthermore, Samsung, in addition to being a smartphone manufacturer, is one of the biggest suppliers of OLED to other phone manufacturers. Samsung would never miss the opportunity to supply to one of the most prominent smartphone brands. Apple is also known for helping its suppliers improve their product quality. An alliance between the two certainly helps Samsung improve the quality of OLED. The coopetition between Apple and Samsung is a win–win for both companies.

Google and Yahoo

In 2015, Yahoo signed a three-year agreement with Google to allow Yahoo to show search results and ads from Google.[4] Google uses a complex set of algorithms to decide which websites to display when a user inputs the search words. Yahoo has been using the Microsoft search engine to power search results. The agreement allowed Yahoo to use Google's search engine in addition to Microsoft's to power its results. Google is required to pay Yahoo for the ad revenue generated through Yahoo. In the process, Google got access to Yahoo users and Yahoo improved the quality of its search engine using Google's search algorithms. The coopetition between the two enhanced revenue for both.

How is Digitalization Helping Coopetition?

Data have become a factor of production in the AI era. Every company needs data to increase productivity, reduce costs and best serve customers. Access to the right kind of data is a challenge for any company. Digitalization is facilitating companies to capture data, use them for further improvements and share them with others. The digitalization of processes is the main driving force behind coopetition among competing parties. Digitalization encourages coopetition by way of sharing mutually useful data, creating shared platforms ecosystem, open source collaboration, open innovation, interoperability, collaborative supply chains, shared customer data and measuring and apportioning benefits to cooperating parties.

For instance, platforms such as 365FarmNet provide an opportunity for competitors to share data for mutual benefit. The coopetition between Google and Yahoo, among telecom companies and among airlines through code sharing has been made possible through the digital process of monitoring the benefit accrued by each party. The number of clicks on an advertisement on Yahoo search results powered by Google can be measured easily through digital means, and the revenue can be apportioned as per the agreed upon terms and conditions.

Ecosystem Approach for Effective Coopetition

The ecosystem approach entails cooperation among all the stakeholders in an industry or sector. For example, the ecosystem for the agricultural sector consists of farmers, farm equipment makers, financial service providers, fertilizer producers, pesticide producers, seed producers, irrigation service providers and weather forecasting services. Similarly, the ecosystem approach in the logistics sector can bring all the logistics service providers—transporters, warehouses, handling agents, distributors, financial service providers, insurers, etc.—on to a single platform. The exchange of information among logistics service providers improves efficiency and ensures success for all the partners. In the ecosystem, all partners are expected to freely exchange data and information through digital integration. The improvement in efficiency, reduction in cost and better service delivery through the ecosystem approach benefit all stakeholders.

Challenges and Opportunities for Leaders of the VUCA World

What is the ecosystem for my industry? How to digitally integrate with other stakeholders?

The challenge before the leaders of the VUCA world is to think beyond their own organization and understand the larger ecosystem they are operating in. The leaders may map all the stakeholders, including competitors, and find ways to mutually benefit each other through digital integration, hence leveraging each other's digital/physical network and monetizing cooperation among different stakeholders. Digital tools may be used for apportioning the revenue generated through mutual cooperation. Leaders would have to identify opportunities for coopetition with their competitors. Business may not always be a zero-sum game where one's gain results in loss for another. Leaders need to emphasize increasing market size through digitalization so that everyone benefits. A control tower approach, as adopted in supply chain management, may be a good option to digitally integrate all stakeholders, including competitors, and derive mutual benefits from coopetition, a unique feature of digitalization.

'The most powerful force ever known on this planet is human cooperation—a force for construction and destruction.'

—Jonathan Haidt

10

Fake Information

'The biggest problem is that Facebook and Google are these giant feedback loops that give people what they want to hear. And when you use them in a world where your biases are being constantly confirmed, you become susceptible to fake news, propaganda, demagoguery.'

—Franklin Foer

ON 30 OCTOBER 1938, CBS RADIO REPORTED AN INVASION OF New Jersey by extraterrestrial beings from Mars. The announcer confirmed that before the invasion, several explosions were reported on Mars' surface. CBS Radio also arranged an interview with Richard Pierson, professor of Astronomy at Princeton, to further investigate the information. He denied any possibility of life on Mars. In the meantime, it was reported that a cylindrical meteorite had landed at Grovers Mill, New Jersey. The radio announcer continued that the cylinder opened and a tentacled, pulsating, barely mobile Martian came out. A policeman approached the Martians with a white handkerchief as a symbol of friendliness, but they emitted some heat rays and killed at least 40 people.

The New Jersey state militia declared martial law and attacked the cylinder. A tripod-like machine emerged from the cylinder and destroyed the army. CBS Radio now started reporting Martians as invaders. The regular news update transformed into an urgent broadcast relaying information about the devastation and evacuation of people. The Martians marched towards New York City, destroying bridges, power stations and railroads on their way. Explosions continued on the Martian surface, and one more cylinder landed in the Great Swamp near Morristown. The Secretary of the Interior addressed the nation to calm down the fear-stricken public. An attempt to bomb a fighting machine by a B-17 bomber also failed. The heat ray from the fighting machine crashed the B-17. The radio reported that the Martians had reached New York City. They used black smoke on the fleeing population. The broadcaster was also killed by the black smoke.

Professor Pierson survived the attack on Grover's Mill. He tried to contact other humans as he wandered through the ruins of New York. To his pleasant surprise, he discovered that the Martians had died. It seemed that they were killed by earthly pathogenic germs, which they were not immune to. Slowly, life became normal.

This infamous incident was broadcasted on the eve of Halloween. Orson Welles had performed—as a part of his radio anthology series *The Mercury Theatre on the Air*—a radio adaptation of H.G. Wells' *The War of the Worlds*, converting the then four-decade-old novel into a fake news bulletin describing a Martian invasion of New Jersey. The broadcast started at 8 p.m. with a disclaimer: 'The following may contain scenes with realistic content, but all viewers need to know is everything you will hear is completely fictional.' Unfortunately, the radio did not consider the audience who turned on their radios late and missed the disclaimer. These listeners took the report to be true and started running for their lives. As reported by news agencies, in a panic, people started looting around the city and crowding the subway stations; gun shops became filled with customers looking to defend themselves. Police lines were choked with continuous calls. The terrified listeners were calling for help, thinking that the world was ending. The impact of this fake news was devastating, even though there was no social media then that could spread any news at lightning speed.

Fake information is not new to humans. Since childhood, we have grown up listening to fake and real stories. In the Hindu epic *Mahabharata*, which is believed to be around 5,000 years old, the Pandavas were finding it impossible to control Dronacharya, the supreme commander of the Kaurava army. Had Dronacharya not stopped, the Pandavas would have fallen. Ashwatthama, Dronacharya's son, was his only weakness. Krishna advised Yudhishthira to lie to Dronacharya that his son had died in the war. Yudhishthira, known for never telling lies, refused to do so. Bhishma found a way to maintain Yudhishthira's truthfulness and trounce Drona. He killed an elephant whose name was also Ashwatthama and shouted, 'Ashwatthama is killed.' Dronacharya got concerned and came to Yudhishthira for the truth. He asked him, 'Is this is true? Is Ashwatthama dead?' Yudhishthira replied, 'Yes, Ashwatthama is dead.' He briefly paused and added under his breath, 'I don't know if it is the man or the elephant.' Drona knew that Yudhishthira never lied and accepted that his son had died. He bowed his head in grief, which led to it being severed.

In the past, the impact of fake information was usually limited to the local area for want of a faster means of communication. However, mass media, such as radio, TV and the internet, have taken the impact of fake news beyond geographical boundaries. The unfortunate broadcast of October 1938, which made people panic, was an eye-opener. Social media has emerged as a boon for those who spread fake information but a bane for netizens. A study by three MIT scholars in 2018 found that false news spreads more rapidly than real news on X (formerly Twitter) and by a substantial margin.[1] The study reported that false news stories are 70 per cent more likely to be retweeted than true stories. It also takes true stories about six times as long as false stories to reach 1,500 people. In the aftermath of the 2016 US presidential election, it was alleged that fake news might have been pivotal in President Donald J. Trump's victory.

In 2016, the World Economic Forum listed digital misinformation as one of the biggest threats to global society. The speed at which news is now distributed is historically unparalleled. Before the internet, we used to get information from magazines, TV and newspapers. Today, anyone can create content and post it on the internet. Generative AI, like ChatGPT, easily produces seemingly authentic content, which enables the creation of misleading or false information. Its ability to mimic human language convincingly raises concerns about the spread of deceptive content. This content can easily be shared on various social media platforms. Fake information, generally sensational, spreads at lightning speed, and we usually trust it without checking its authenticity. While the information in traditional media was filtered by editors, there is no filter for the information created on social media.

For example, the spread of COVID-19 since December 2019 led to a global pandemic that claimed many lives. This period witnessed the spread of misinformation about the origin, effects and cure of the disease. The spread of misleading information about the virus led the WHO to warn the masses of an ongoing infodemic and an overabundance of information, especially misinformation, during the pandemic.[2]

Deepfake

Deepfake is a type of AI technology that uses ML algorithms to simulate neural networks with massive datasets to create fake videos or images that appear to be real. In 2018, a potential misuse of deepfakes was demonstrated by Jordan Peele, an American comedian, who created a deepfake video of former President Barack Obama commenting on the then US President Trump. This showed that deepfake technology has the potential to be used for propaganda, misinformation and other malicious purposes. The widespread integration of AI has led to a drastic surge in deepfake-related scams. According to Sumsub, a UK-based verification platform, there has been a remarkable tenfold rise in identified deepfakes worldwide across various sectors between 2022 and 2023.[3] Some recent cases of deepfakes in India are presented here.

Rashmika Mandanna Deepfake Case (November 2023)

A malicious deepfake video featuring actress Rashmika Mandanna ignited a storm of anger and fear in India in November 2023. The AI-powered manipulation, which convincingly placed her face on another woman's body, exposed the chilling potential of weaponizing this technology. The incident sparked an important conversation about online safety and the vulnerability of public figures in the AI era.

On 20 January 2024, Delhi Police arrested a 24-year-old BTech graduate, Eemani Naveen, from Andhra Pradesh's Guntur district for creating the deepfake video of Mandanna.[4] Naveen, a work-from-home video editor and social media manager, confessed that his motive was to boost followers on an Instagram channel he had dedicated to the Bollywood star. This case is more than a personal attack on one individual. It serves as a stark reminder of the potential for deepfakes to be used for malicious purposes, from damaging reputations to manipulating public opinion or even influencing elections.

Sachin Tendulkar Fake Video Case (January 2024)

On 15 January 2024, legendary Indian cricketer Sachin Tendulkar shared on X (formerly Twitter) that a fake video of him was being circulated online. In the video, he is found promoting a gaming app, claiming that his daughter Sara is able to easily earn huge sums of money by playing the game, but Sachin clarified that it's not real. He tweeted, 'These videos are fake. It is disturbing to see rampant misuse of technology. Request everyone to report videos, ads & apps like these in large numbers. Social Media platforms need to be alert and responsive to complaints. Swift action from their end is crucial to stopping the spread of misinformation and deepfakes.'[5]

In a culturally diverse country like India, deepfakes can also be used to create mistrust among different religious groups. For instance, deepfakes can be used to create false information and conspiracy theories to harm the relationship among different communities. We need to be wary of the potential impact of deepfakes on society and ensure that they do not promote or encourage the spread of misinformation.

The consequences of the spread of deepfakes in a diverse country are significant and can lead to violence, riots or civil unrest. Therefore, leaders must monitor the spread of deepfakes and develop effective strategies to counter their impact.

Data Integrity: A Challenge

Data integrity refers to the accuracy, consistency (validity) and reliability of data over their life cycle. Compromised data are of no use to enterprises, not to mention the dangers of the loss of sensitive data. Data has become one of the factors of production along with land, labour, capital and entrepreneurship. Accenture's Technology Vision 2018 report found that 79 per cent of organizations today base their most critical systems and decisions on data, yet many do not invest in the capabilities to verify the truth within them.[6] How can an enterprise productively use any factor of production if it is not trustworthy? Indeed, data integrity is emerging as one of the biggest challenges in the data-driven economy. Sellers often pay people to submit favourable fake reviews of products and services. 'Likes' for Facebook posts can be bought online. Organizations using social media data for trend analysis and demand prediction need to be wary of the risks of fake data.

Allegedly, there are millions of fake or bot accounts on X (erstwhile Twitter). It is believed to have deleted 70 million fake and suspicious accounts in May and June 2018. In April 2022, Elon Musk, among the richest persons in the world, surprised the stock market by announcing his intention to buy the Twitter platform, which the latter agreed to for $44 billion. This euphoria was rather short-lived. On 13 May 2022, Musk tweeted that the deal was on hold due to a lack of information on spam/fake accounts. Twitter claimed that spam and bot accounts make up less than 5 per cent of its total users, whereas Elon believed that they could account for 20 per cent or more of Twitter users. Finally, on 27 October 2022, Elon announced that he had closed the deal and bought Twitter and subsequently renamed it as X. Despite relentless efforts, X is still believed to be grappling with the problem of fake accounts.

Considering the challenges posed by fake information, the UK government in August 2024 announced its plan to introduce a new curriculum to help students identify and avoid fake news.[7] This initiative is part of a broader effort to enhance media literacy among young people, equipping them with the critical thinking skills needed to navigate misinformation online. The curriculum will include lessons on recognizing biased sources, understanding the role of algorithms in spreading misinformation, and verifying the authenticity of information. The goal is to better prepare students to discern credible information in an increasingly complex digital landscape.

Challenges and Opportunities for Leaders of the VUCA World

How to detect fake data?

Leaders need to be vigilant about the veracity of data being used for making decisions. This is easier said than done. They must look at the source, context and integrity of data.

Data may be sourced from external agencies or internal business processes. Data from a third party should be verified before being used. For example, the demand forecast from a retailer may be inflated to get priority in supply. The supplier needs to verify demand from the actual sales figures. Internal data, although more likely to be trustworthy, should also undergo verification.

Leaders should also ensure that the data are used only for the context they have been collected for. Data should also be relevant to the time frame they are being used in. For example, the data for international travel demand during the COVID-19 pandemic, when the world was under severe travel restrictions, are not useful to predict demand in the post-pandemic world. So, context and time frame are important to decide whether the data are trustworthy.

Further, leaders should ensure data integrity through stringent cybersecurity measures. If data integrity is violated due to some cyberattack, the compromised data are garbage. Decisions taken based on compromised data can never be prudent.

Leaders may use the SMELL test to differentiate between fake and real information. The SMELL test was first introduced by McManus in 2013 in his article titled 'Don't Be Fooled: Use the SMELL Test to Separate Fact from Fiction Online' for consumers to appraise news and claims in the media and on social media.[8] This a tool for vetting news and information in the AI era. It has gained immense importance in the age of information explosion to discern facts from fiction.

The mnemonic version of the SMELL test introduced by McManus is as follows:

> **S** stands for **Source**. Who is providing the information?
> **M** is for **Motivation**. Why are they telling me this?
> **E** represents **Evidence**. What evidence is provided for generalizations?
> **L** is for **Logic**. Do the facts logically compel the conclusions?
> **L** is for **Left out**. What's missing that might change our interpretation of the information?

Source

This refers to who or what is providing the information and whether they are reliable and trustworthy. Is the information first-hand or hearsay? Are the sources free from conflicts of interest? Do the sources have appropriate knowledge and experience on the topic? Content from anonymous sources cannot be trusted.

Motivation

Understanding the motivation behind a source is important for distinguishing between those who provide information and those who are seeking to persuade. Persuaders often selectively present facts that support their viewpoint, while true information providers offer a balanced perspective, covering all relevant sides of an issue. Leaders must, therefore, assess the intent behind the information, data or news they receive.

Evidence

What is the factual evidence for the information? Has the information been verified, or can it be verified? Has the information been correctly interpreted? Is it backed by credible, evidence-based sources?

Logic

Does the information make logical sense? Does the logic match the context? Is the conclusion backed by evidence? Leaders need to look for overgeneralizations and erroneous comparisons, especially correlation vs causation.

Left Out

Leaders may find out what information has not been provided, either intentionally or unintentionally, and why. The left-out information may change the context and interpretation. Is only one side of the story presented?

Conclusively, the SMELL test can be a very effective tool for analysing the trustworthiness of information. Leaders will have to put it in practice sooner rather than later.

The opportunity before leaders is to outshine others when it comes to finding the trustworthiness of information/data. A decision taken based on fake data may be disastrous for an organization. Leaders who are able to differentiate between real and fake will win the race in the AI era.

'We can't have like willy-nilly proliferation of fake news, that's crazy. You can't have more types of fake news than real news. That's allowing public deception to go unchecked. That's crazy.'

—Elon Musk

11

Personalization: The 5th P of Marketing

*'I'm most passionate about personalization.
I firmly believe that personalized experiences with
brands will most drive loyalty and relevance
for customers in the future.'*

—Katrina Lake

MICHAEL DELL WAS BORN IN 1965 IN HOUSTON, TEXAS. SINCE childhood, he displayed a knack for entrepreneurship. As a 12-year-old, he traded stamps and basketball cards through the mail and earned $2,000. At the age of 14, he got his first computer, Apple II. His insatiable quest for knowledge about computers led him to take it apart, which he then reassembled to understand how the different components were put together. He realized that computers can be easily assembled using components that can be obtained from different sources such as hardware shops, individual equipment manufacturers and electronic retail shops. His parents wanted him to become a doctor because his father was an orthodontist. As per his parents' wishes, he entered the University of Texas at Austin in 1983, but his interest was in computers. He realized that there existed a huge opportunity in assembling and selling computers directly to customers at much cheaper prices than those of established brands like IBM. He once explained to Richard Murphy of *Success* magazine[1]:

> I saw that you'd buy a PC for about $3,000, and inside that PC was about $600 worth of parts. IBM would buy most of these parts from other companies, assemble them, and sell the computer to a dealer for $2,000. Then the dealer, who knew very little about selling or supporting computers, would sell it for $3,000, which was even more outrageous.

When well-known brands such as IBM and Apple were investing heavily in maintaining expensive inventory and selling their standard computers through a chain of retailers, Dell introduced the most innovative business model called Dell Direct, which involved selling the computers directly to customers without any retailer. The principle behind the direct model was to improve efficiency by removing layers of intermediaries, and directly connecting with the customer. The model's USP was the personalization of the computers as per the needs of the individual customers. The competitors were selling a limited range of computer models, and the customers had no choice but to select from the available models. Many times, customers had to unnecessarily spend for the expensive configurations of computers because the configurations they needed were not available. Dell could envision an opportunity for personalization in the burgeoning computer market. He advertised his computers in the leading magazines focused on computers. Customers could send their request and desired configuration by phone or fax. Dell would assemble the computer as per the configuration specified by the customer and ship it to them. The proliferation of internet services was a boon for Dell's direct model. In 1996, he started selling personal computers (PCs) online. He also offered customer support through the internet. Dell soon emerged as one of the largest sellers of computers in the world.

The customized configuration of the computers was the key to the success of the Dell direct model. Such customization of expensive products as per customers' requirements is not unknown in history. Indeed, before the Industrial Revolution, products were made by hand as per the order. Till the introduction of the assembly line by Henry Ford in 1913, every car was produced differently as per the customer's order. In the post-world war era, factories powered by electricity were booming, mechanization and automation were leading the production lines, and the mass-scale production of standard products became the norm. Until the late nineties, before the widespread adoption of ready-made clothes, clothes were stitched only by trained tailors. These tailors would take precise measurements of individuals to ensure a perfect fit. The mass production of standard-size clothes in factories replaced tailors.

Digitalization Paving the Way for Personalization

The personalization of computers by Dell in the era of mass production was a paradigm shift. Dell's success is largely attributed to the internet boom: the convenience of configuring computers online, placing orders online and paying online from the comfort of the home. Personalization is the new word in the marketing lexicon. Philip Kotler, the father of modern marketing, describes the marketing mix—the four Ps of marketing—as product, price, place and promotion. One of the first steps in marketing is customer segmentation based on a number of factors such as age, gender, education, income, occupation and preferences. The marketing strategy has to be targeted to individual customers to be effective. Every individual behaves differently irrespective of the customer segment they belong to.

In the AI era, companies are able to track every customer's preferences based on what they do on the internet, including their purchasing, browsing and watching activities. When you accept 'cookies' on any website, you are allowing it to track your browsing activities. Our every action is being watched and processed by these companies to understand us better. Based on the collected data, companies offer personalized recommendations to individuals.

The enigmatic question of 'Who am I?' has remained an unsolved mystery for ages. However, in today's AI era, the internet knows who you are, your activities and your preferences and aversions. In 2012, *The New York Times* published a story titled 'How Companies Learn Your Secrets'.[2] The story talked about a prediction model developed by Target Corporation, an American chain of departmental stores, to predict its customers' pregnancy status. As per the story, after one year of deploying the model, a man stormed into a Minneapolis-based Target retail store and questioned the manager about how he dared to send coupons to buy baby stuff to his daughter. 'My daughter got this in the mail!' he said. 'She's still in high school, and you're sending her coupons for baby clothes and cribs? Are you trying to encourage her to get pregnant?' The manager was clueless about what was happening. He checked the sent emails to find that they were indeed sent to his daughter; they contained advertisements for maternity clothing and nursery furniture and pictures of smiling infants. The manager was embarrassed and apologized to the man. A few days later, the manager called the father to apologize again. However, to his surprise, the father apologized to him. 'I had a talk with my daughter,' he said. 'It turns out there've been some activities in my house I haven't been completely aware of. She's due in August. I owe you an apology.' It turned out that Target's prediction model knew more about the daughter than the father. It is not known whether this is a true story, but it is possible. The fact remains that machines may know us better than we know ourselves.

Personalization is the fifth weapon in the arsenal of the marketing mix to effectively woo customers in the AI era. Personalization has become central to the other Ps of the marketing mix. The product, the first P of the mix, has to be customized as per the personal needs of an individual customer after monitoring their preferences online. Then it has to be placed (the second P) in the traditional marketplace or on an online platform where that specific customer usually browses. The product has to be promoted (the third P) on websites and mobile apps where the targeted customer would not miss the advertisements. The advertising is personalized and targeted at the individual customer. The product should be priced (the fourth P) as per the purchase history of the specific customer (it is not uncommon in the AI era that the same product is priced differently for different customers depending upon their spending history).

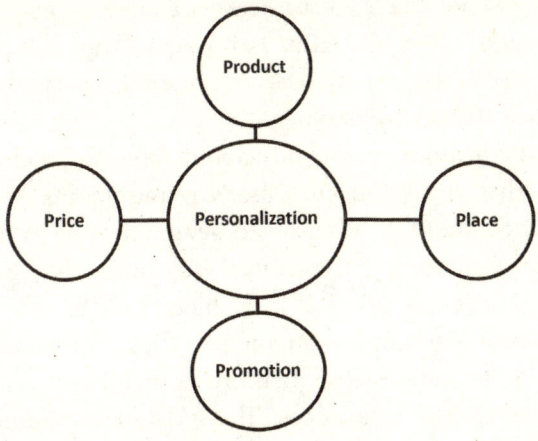

Figure 11.1: Personalization: The 5th P of marketing

Challenges and Opportunities for Leaders of the VUCA World

How to offer a personalized experience to customers digitally?

In the fast-paced VUCA world, customer expectations are evolving rapidly. Today's customers expect a personalized experience that caters to their unique needs and preferences. The challenge for leaders is to leverage digital technologies to offer such personalized experiences to their customers.

Digitalization has made it possible to gather a vast amount of data on individual customers. Their likes and dislikes can be monitored using data about their past purchases or online browsing history. Even seasonality in demand can be assessed based on month-wise sales data for different products. By analysing these data, businesses can understand their customers' preferences and create personalized offerings. This has opened up a world of opportunities for businesses to provide a customized experience to every customer.

Personalization is not only about offering products or services that meet the customer's requirements but also about understanding the customer's journey and pain points and offering personalized solutions that address their specific needs. Digital technologies make it possible to track and trace every interaction that a customer has with the organization from their browsing history, purchase history, queries or grievances. These data can be analysed to create a customer persona, which can then be used to create tailored products.

Digital platforms such as Amazon, Netflix and Booking.com have already mastered the art of personalization. These platforms use sophisticated algorithms to analyse customer data and offer personalized recommendations. For instance, Amazon recommends products based on the customer's purchase history and browsing behaviour, and Netflix recommends movies and TV shows based on the viewer's watch history.

Every business now has an opportunity to differentiate itself from its competitors and offer a unique value proposition to its customers. Personalization can lead to higher customer loyalty, repeat business and increased revenue.

Personalization is a critical component of the VUCA world. Digital technologies offer an unprecedented opportunity to create personalized experiences for customers at a fraction of the cost. Leaders who can leverage these technologies to offer customized solutions will be the winners in a highly competitive business environment. Never before has such an opportunity be used to reach customers individually at throwaway prices.

> *'Over the years, the internet has been going down the path of becoming a more personalized experience.'*
>
> —Alan Schaaf

12

The Safety of Humans

'Self-driving cars are the natural extension of active safety and obviously something we should do.'

—Elon Musk

ON 4 SEPTEMBER, 2022, CYRUS MISTRY'S DEATH DUE TO A ROAD accident shocked the entire nation. Cyrus Pallonji Mistry, former chairman of Tata Sons, India, and managing director of the Shapoorji Pallonji Group, died under unfortunate circumstances in a road accident while travelling from Gujarat's Udwada to Mumbai. He was riding in the back seat with Jehangir Pandole, a former Indian national squash champion. Dr Anahita Pandole, a prominent gynaecologist from Mumbai, was driving, and her husband, Darius Pandole, was in the front passenger seat when the accident occurred. While attempting to overtake another vehicle from the wrong side at around 2.30 p.m. on the fateful day, the car hit the road divider on the bridge over the Surya river at Charoti Naka. The impact was so severe that Jehangir and Mistry, who were not wearing seat belts, died on the spot, while Anahita and Darius suffered serious injuries. The investigation revealed that the airbags in the front seats opened and protected the occupants because they were wearing their seat belts, but the airbags in the rear seats did not deploy because Mistry and Jehangir were not wearing seat belts. According to the car's airbag system design, airbags deploy only when the seat belts are fastened. In November 2022, Anahita Pandole was booked by the police for multiple driving offences, including causing death due to negligence, rash driving, overspeeding, overtaking, not following lane discipline and ignoring the rules that a driver should follow.[1] Conclusively, a sum of the human errors of overspeeding, overtaking from the wrong side, and rear seat occupants not using the seat belts caused the unfortunate death of a legendary businessman in India. The incident drew worldwide media attention due to the high-profile victims. Unfortunately, fatalities in road accidents caused by human error are not uncommon.

As per the data provided in the 'Road Accidents in India 2022' report, more than 0.17 million people were killed and 0.44 million were injured in 0.46 million road accidents in India in 2022.[2] On average, 462 deaths occur every day due to road accidents, a whopping 19 deaths per hour. Data further reveal human error, including traffic rule violation, driving without a valid driver licence and the non-use of safety devices, as the major cause of road accidents in India. Around 72.3 per cent of road accidents caused by traffic rule violation occurred due to overspeeding, followed by driving on the wrong side (4.9 per cent). The situation is not very different even in developed countries. More than 35,000 people die each year in road accidents in the US. A 2016 study by the National Highway Transportation Safety Administration, USA, found that human error accounts for around 94 per cent of all road accidents.[3]

Individuals who are driving seem to be the single most reason for fatalities in road accidents. The question arises whether humans are safe drivers. Tesla and SpaceX founder Elon Musk opined that humans will eventually no longer be allowed to drive cars because they are not good enough at it. At Nvidia's annual developers' conference in 2015, he said that 'Artificial intelligence can do a much better job than humans', and that 'It's too dangerous; you can't have a person driving a two-tonne death machine'.[4] Self-driving or autonomous cars are claimed to be safer than human-driven ones as autonomous vehicles can react faster than human drivers. These cars do not drive drunk, text while driving or even get tired. In the future, humans may not even be allowed to drive vehicles. It is not a utopian thought. In the metro rail industry, driverless train operations technology is already replacing human drivers to run trains safely and efficiently at closer headway. Most modern airplanes are equipped with autopilot mode, which is capable of controlling the aircraft without the pilot directly operating the controls. The general guidance given to pilots is to let the computer do it because it can do a better job than a human.

Rio Tinto, a leading Australian mining company, operates autonomous trucks as part of the autonomous haulage system for mining iron from hazardous mines. For over a decade, automation has played a significant role in Rio Tinto's business, enabling the company to operate in a safer, more efficient and cost-effective manner. The company has been able to eliminate human drivers' errors and enhance safety just by increasing the level of automation in its trucks, drills and trains. Rio Tinto claims, 'In 2018, each truck was estimated to have operated on average 700 hours more than conventional haul trucks, with 15 per cent lower costs, delivering clear productivity benefits.'[5]

Industries are increasingly adopting automation not only to improve productivity but also to ensure the safety of their employees and surrounding life forms, especially in hazardous sectors. Automation is no longer an option but has become essential for the safety of human beings.

Automation, Digitalization and Robotics for Safety

Automation is not new for humans. Watermills were used by the Greeks and Romans for grinding grain into flour around the first century BC. What is new is digitalization, which is driving automation today. In fact, nowadays, digitalization is regarded as the first step towards automation. Digitalized information then becomes the input for the system that is to be automated. For example, IoT sensors first convert the collected information into data, pre-process them (if required) and then feed the data into the automation application.

The history of the successful development of robotics is closely linked to digitalization. In 1950, the early-age robots were industrial machines deployed on the assembly line for specific tasks such as cutting, welding, painting and assembling. Unimate was the first such robot deployed by General Motors in the 1960s at a New Jersey plant for the transportation of die castings from an assembly line and welding these parts on auto bodies; this was considered a hazardous task for workers. The 1970s witnessed second-generation robots equipped with sensors that enabled them to react to their environment. Third-generation robots, developed in 1980–2000, were reprogrammable and used digital technologies. These robots were used by many industrial sectors for various activities such as welding, painting, soldering, moving and assembling. Third-generation robots were able to perform all kinds of tasks they were programmed for but lacked 'intelligence' and 'reason'. From 2000 onwards, the era of smart digital robotics started. Recent developments in AI, speech recognition, computer vision and neural networks have paved the way for truly intelligent robots that can take verbal commands, recognize things, think, understand and work like human beings to some extent. These fourth-generation intelligent robots are swiftly taking over hazardous work environments, displacing humans in the process. For instance, in nuclear power plants and chemical factories, these advanced robotic systems are assuming roles that were traditionally performed by humans, thus ensuring safety and efficiency.

Challenges and Opportunities for Leaders of the VUCA World

How to improve the safety of employees and others using automation and digitalization?

Automation has revolutionized the way businesses operate, and its role in boosting human safety cannot be overstated. Due to the rapid progress in technology, numerous tasks that were once deemed safe to carry out manually are now being classified as unsafe. A prime illustration of this shift is the perception that the automated operations of metro trains, such as driverless systems, are safer than their manual counterparts.

This means that leaders need to prioritize the adoption of automation to improve the safety of employees and customers alike. If they fail to do so, automation may soon be forced upon them by policymakers and regulatory boards.

One of the main challenges faced by leaders in this regard is finding ways to implement automation for safety as soon as possible. They need to act fast and ensure that their employees and customers are protected from harm by using automated solutions that can perform the same tasks more efficiently and with fewer risks. For instance, the auto industry has been equipping vehicles with more and more safety features to keep customers safe. Safety features such as electronic stability control, lane-keeping assist, cruise control and autonomous emergency braking system are included in most cars today.

Automation enhances safety and improves the efficiency of business operations. By automating hazardous tasks, leaders can ensure that their employees are focused on more critical but less dangerous tasks. The use of automated solutions not only reduces the chances of accidents but also saves businesses time and money, thereby allowing them to achieve more with less.

Despite the many benefits of automation, leaders must be prepared to face resistance from employees who may view automation as a threat to their jobs. This fear is understandable, but leaders must take steps to allay these fears and ensure that employees understand that automation is being introduced for their safety and to make their work more efficient, not to replace them.

The adoption of automation for safety and efficiency presents an opportunity for companies to gain a competitive advantage over their competitors. They can boast about their safety record and showcase their adoption of automation as evidence of their responsible approach towards human safety. The use of automation can also help businesses avoid costly accidents and mitigate the risk of potential lawsuits, ensuring that they remain profitable in the long run.

'The automation of automation, the automation of intelligence, is such an incredible idea that if we could continue to improve this capability, the applications are really quite boundless.'

—Jensen Huang

13

Fraud Detection and Prevention

'With commerce comes fraud.'
—Nathan Blecharczyk

Dear friend,

Please forgive me for stressing you with this mail, as I know that my mail will come to you as a surprise. I am Mr. Jeppe Tranholm-Mikkelsen, 52 years old, from Burkina Faso in West Africa. I am a banker by profession and currently occupying the position of Audits and Account Manager, Société Générale, Burkina Faso. I have a business proposal to the tune of $8.5 million for you to handle with me. I have the opportunity to transfer this abandoned fund, which belongs to one of our late clients who died in an accident with his family, to your bank account in your country. Since his death, the fund has been in a suspended account because none of his family survived to lay claim to the fund. Due to the statistics of this fund, I want you to apply to the bank as the next of kin to the fund, so that our bank will give you recognition and have the funds transferred into your account. As a banker in this bank, I have the opportunity to transfer this abandoned fund to your bank account in your country without any hindrance if only

> you will give me your 100 per cent assurance that you can handle this transaction deal. However, further details of this transaction and the text of the request form will be sent to you upon receipt of your response. We will also discuss the percentage sharing. Please kindly reply to me if you are interested in this transaction as I await your immediate response when you receive this mail. You can reply to me through my private email: info.m.jeppe@gmail.com
>
> Thanks.
> Jeppe Tranholm-Mikkelsen
> whatsappPh+......

Many readers would have received such an email. Of course, such business proposals are fake and aimed at gullible new internet or email users who often fall prey to these fraudulent messages. Also called 419 fraud, advance-fee scam or Nigerian letter scam, it is one of the most common scams on the internet. The scam has earned its name after the Nigerian criminal code-419 that outlaws fraud. The modus operandi entails the fraudster sending a mail claiming to be a member of a wealthy family or a banker from Nigeria or any other African country. The person claims to be in possession of a large sum of money left by someone wealthy and seeks your help to relocate this fortune out of the country for safekeeping and into your bank account, or offers some business opportunity to invest that money. However, you are requested to deposit a small payment as a fee in return for the large chunk of payment promised by the fraudster, which, of course, you will never receive.

Lottery Scam

> Dear Winner,
>
> The Microsoft Millions Lottery is proud to inform you that you have won (£950,000.00, NINE HUNDRED AND FIFTY THOUSAND POUNDS ONLY) from Microsoft Promotion in conjunction with Nokia Cell Phone Award. Your email address is one of (9) lucky ones to have won the Microsoft Millions Lottery Campaign Weekly Promotion, and we wish to congratulate you on your victory.

This is another kind of fraud called a lottery scam. You will be declared the winner of a lottery organized by some reputed firm and will be asked to deposit tax before receiving the lottery amount. Sure enough, you will never receive the lottery amount and will also lose your money that you thought was deposited as tax.

Most smart readers like you would think that no sensible person can be fooled by these obviously fake emails. Well, as per the FBI Internet Crime Report 2021, more than 11,000 people reported falling victim to advance-fee scams in the US in 2021, losing around $100 million.[1] If this is the situation in a developed country with supposedly high-level internet literacy, the plight of those with minimal or zero e-literacy cannot even be imagined.

The targets of online fraud are not just nouveau internet users; even well-established companies fall prey to them. The Association of Certified Fraud Executives in the US has estimated that organizations worldwide lose around 5 per cent of revenue or $4 trillion to fraud every year.

Business leaders are routinely challenged by online

fraudsters to protect their businesses and customers. If a customer is cheated through some online scam, the business cannot transfer the responsibility of the loss to the customer, even if the fraud has happened because of the customer's carelessness or naivety. Businesses must take the onus of proactively making customers aware of possible frauds and informing them of the preventive measures to be taken to protect themselves from these frauds. Some ways in which businesses use digital technologies to detect and prevent fraud are discussed below.

Data Analytics to Prevent Frauds

The biggest advantage of using data analytics for fraud detection is its ability to process huge amounts of data very fast, almost in real time. The data can help find areas most prone to fraud and can be studied to take preemptive measures to prevent fraud. Data analytics helps analyse trends and find patterns much faster than humans who use conventional methods, such as spreadsheets and comparative analysis, to study the data. For example, in the credit card business, protection from fraud is fundamental to gain a competitive advantage. A credit card company that is vulnerable to fraud cannot stay in the business for long. Credit card companies use data analytics to prevent fraudulent transactions. They analyse consumer credit card usage behaviour to train an ML model. The ML model is then used to detect any fraudulent transaction that does not conform to the usual pattern of the customer's credit card usage. For example, frequent high-value transactions may seem suspicious and are promptly verified by the credit card company. Another important factor is the location of the IP address. If the same credit card is used from multiple IP addresses from different locations across the world, it might have been hacked and is instantly blocked to prevent further fraud.

Forensic Data Analytics

Digitalization is helping businesses develop intelligence to investigate fraud. A new field of study has emerged: forensic data analytics (FDA), which refers to the study of digital data and investigation of cybercrime. Financial institutions and insurance companies are perhaps the largest users of FDA. It facilitates businesses to search for patterns in behaviour, actions and movement of money. It helps investigate and prevent fraud by integrating ML capabilities with learnings from the forensic investigation of fraudsters' motives and methods.

Fraud Within the Organization

Fraud, data theft and security breaches are grave risks faced by organizations in the AI era. There is no longer a need to access physical files, take photocopies of confidential papers, and hide them in big bags to take them out of company premises. Information worth thousands of physical files, if available in digital form, can be downloaded in a small chip or transferred online within seconds. Inventions/Designs/Drawings/Intellectual property rights, etc. are prone to such fraudulent breaches if not secured.

In one such case of fraud within the organization, an

ex-Apple worker was arrested for stealing self-driving car trade secrets in 2018.[2] Xiaolang Zhang was working in Apple's autonomous car division. His job involved creating software and hardware for Apple's autonomous vehicle initiative. He was responsible for designing and testing circuit boards that would analyse sensor data. In April 2018, he travelled to China on paternity leave. On his return, he informed his supervisor of his intention to resign and move to China to work for Xiaopeng Motors, an intelligent electric vehicle company headquartered in China. Apple security officials found that Zhang had searched Apple's secret database while he was on paternity leave. He downloaded data, including a 25-page secret blueprint of a circuit board for a self-driving car, to his personal laptop. When confronted, Zhang owned up to stealing company data. The case was referred to the FBI for further investigation, and Zhang was charged with stealing trade secrets. Alert Apple officials could save their confidential data from being accessed by the company's competitors, but everyone may not be so fortunate. A proactive approach to monitoring the logs of databases, learning from usual patterns and detecting any suspicious activity using data analytics may be essential to prevent fraud within the organization.

Challenges and Opportunities for Leaders of the VUCA World

How to devise digital methods to prevent fraud in organizations?

In today's fast-paced AI era, frauds and scams are becoming increasingly common. With the rise of digitalization, cybercriminals are finding new and sophisticated ways to carry out fraudulent activities. From identity theft to phishing scams, fraudsters are always on the lookout for new ways to exploit the vulnerabilities of the AI era. The onus is on the leaders of the VUCA world to be vigilant and protect their customers and organizations from the devastating consequences of digital fraud.

Preventing hacking and protecting confidential data is more imperative now than ever before. To safeguard against fraud, leaders need to be proactive and take a strategic approach to manage the risks associated with digitalization. They need to be aware of the possible vulnerabilities in their digital infrastructure and continuously monitor their systems. This involves a comprehensive risk assessment of the potential risks, their impact and the likelihood of each risk event.

One way to combat digital fraud is using data analytics to detect and prevent fraudulent activities. Data analytics can help identify patterns and anomalies that may indicate fraudulent activity. This can include tracking unusual login attempts, large transactions or suspicious behaviour. By analysing customer behaviour and transaction patterns, leaders can identify potential fraudsters and take appropriate action to prevent further damage.

Moreover, leaders can use AI and ML to build predictive models that can help detect frauds before they occur. These models can be built on vast amounts of data collected from various sources, including social media, customer interactions and transaction histories. Using these models, leaders can predict and prevent fraudulent activity with high accuracy. It is important that employees are trained to recognize and respond to fraudulent activities and are responsible for protecting the organization and its customers.

The opportunities lie in establishing an organization with robust anti-fraud measures that minimize susceptibility to fraudulent activities. This fosters greater trust and integrity, creating a competitive edge. Businesses can attract new customers, strengthen stakeholder confidence, explore untapped markets and enhance long-term sustainability. Leaders who are able to tap into this opportunity will be able to sail through the tsunamis of digital fraud and succeed in the end.

'It is always right to detect a fraud, and to perceive a folly, but it is very often wrong to expose either. A man of business should always have his eyes open but must often seem to have them shut.'

—Philip Stanhope

14

Data Security

*'No technology that's connected
to the internet is unhackable.'*

—Abhijit Naskar

Colonial Pipeline Cyberattack

ON 7 MAY 2021, THE COLONIAL PIPELINE, A CRITICAL infrastructure system in the US, faced the largest known cyberattack in the history of the oil and gas distribution system.[1] The hackers, identified as DarkSide, were able to access the pipeline's IT network and steal around 100 GB of data, affecting billing, accounting and many other computerized systems. The organization's management decided to shut down the operations of the pipeline to prevent the ransomware from spreading further.

The Colonial Pipeline is the largest pipeline system (8,850 km) for refined oil products in the US. It carries around 460 million litres of fuel per day between Texas and New York.

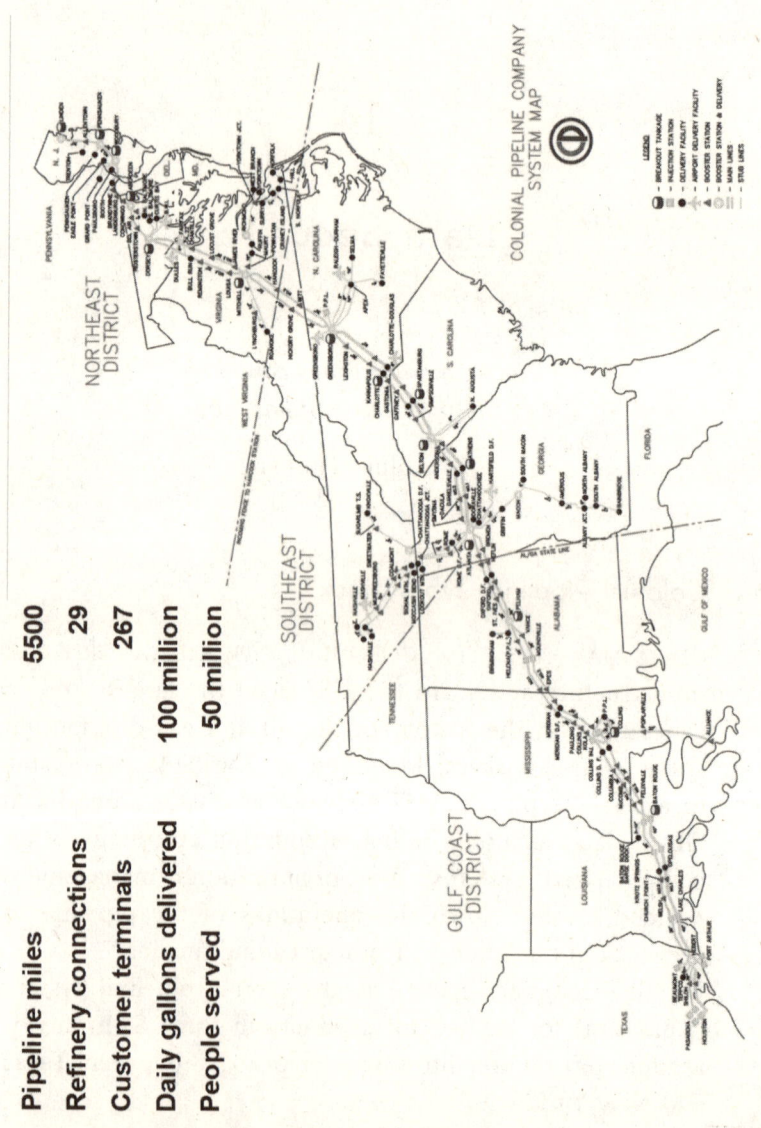

The Colonial Pipeline network[2]

The sudden closure of the Colonial Pipeline severely impacted oil supply in many eastern states of the US. There was a shortage of jet fuel for airlines. Panic buying of gas was observed at gas stations, causing a spike in the gas price. On 9 May 2021, the US Federal Motor Carrier Safety Administration issued a regional emergency declaration for 17 states and Washington, DC, to keep fuel supply lines open.[3] The hackers were paid $4.4 million in the form of 75 bitcoin to retrieve the data and make the pipeline operational again on 12 May 2021.

During the congressional hearing, Colonial Pipeline CEO Joseph Blount informed the US Senate committee that the system was attacked using a legacy virtual private network (VPN). The system could be accessed through the one-step verification of a password. This meant that Colonial Pipeline's IT system could be accessed directly through a password without second-step authentication, such as a text message, OTP or hardware token.

Later, the US Department of Justice's Ransomware and Digital Extortion Task Force was able to trace the digital address of the account that the attackers used for collecting the ransom and recovered 64 of the 75 bitcoin paid by Colonial Pipeline.

The case exposes the vulnerability of IT networks to cyberattacks. It is not an isolated data breach incident but a publicly disclosed high-profile case. It was indeed an eye-opener for business leaders as well as the government.

Trains Halted in Denmark

On 29 October 2022, the Danish State Railway (Danske

Statsbaner or DSB) had to stop its train services for several hours due to a cyberattack.[4] DSB is Denmark's largest train operator and operates only passenger trains. The ransomware attacked the IT system of Supeo, a Danish company responsible for providing asset management solutions to DSB. Supeo provides a mobile application to DSB train drivers to access safety-critical information such as speed restrictions and track blockage due to maintenance works. The train drivers need this vital information to control the speed of trains at locations under speed restrictions or to stop the train before the maintenance location. Any error in this information may cause an accident. Due to the cyberattack, the mobile application used by the train drivers to access this information was compromised. To ensure the safety of train operations, Supeo decided to shut down its servers; the application stopped working, and drivers were forced to stop their trains.

Ransomware Attack on All India Institute of Medical Sciences

On 23 November 2022, e-Hospital services at the All India Institute of Medical Sciences (AIIMS) were crippled for nearly two weeks because of ransomware attacks. As the servers were down, the hospital's outpatient and inpatient digital services, smart lab, billing, report generation and appointment system were unavailable. The sensitive medical data of more than 30 million patients were believed to have been compromised.[5] Media reports indicated that the attackers demanded a ransom of INR 2 billion to restore the data.

It is believed that an AIIMS employee clicked on a web link embedded in a gaming or similar website a few months before and malware was downloaded on to his computer. In the absence of any secured cyber firewall or other protections, the malware infected other computers and servers. The attackers got access to the AIIMS servers through this malware, downloaded the sensitive data and encrypted them to prevent their use by the AIIMS IT system. Finally, on 16 December 2022, it was reported that all the data for the e-Hospital were retrieved from a backup server, which was unaffected, and restored on new servers.[6]

NotPetya: The Global Cyber Catastrophe

On 27 June 2017, a cyberattack known as NotPetya began in Ukraine.[7] It started like many other cyberattacks, with the malware spreading through a routine software update from a popular Ukrainian accounting software called MeDoc. However, what made NotPetya different was its devastating reach and impact.

At first, the malware appeared to be ransomware, demanding a bitcoin payment to unlock infected computers, but NotPetya was far more destructive. It wasn't designed to make money but to cause chaos. It used a tool called EternalBlue—originally developed by the U.S. National Security Agency to exploit a vulnerability in Microsoft Windows that allowed users to gain access to computers connected to a network. It was later leaked and the malware spread quickly through networks. Once it infiltrated a system, it moved from one computer to another, causing widespread damage.

NotPetya, named for its similarity to the ransomware Petya, emerged in 2017 with a destructive twist. Unlike Petya, which extorted victims for a decryption key, NotPetya's ransom messages were a façade. Its true purpose was to irreversibly encrypt master boot records, thus rendering computers inoperable.

One of the hardest-hit companies was Maersk, a global shipping giant. Almost overnight, Maersk found itself in a crisis. Its operations came to a standstill, and it had to reinstall 4,000 servers, 45,000 PCs and 2,500 applications just to get back on track. This process took weeks and significantly disrupted its business.

Merck, a major pharmaceutical company, was also impacted. Its production lines were halted and research projects were delayed. The attack affected its ability to manufacture and distribute medications, highlighting the real-world consequences of cyberattacks on public health.

FedEx's TNT Express was another major victim. As a logistics company, its operations depend on precise timing and coordination. NotPetya threw its schedules into disarray, causing delays and financial losses.

The financial damage NotPetya caused was enormous and estimated to be around $10 billion. However, the cost went beyond money. Businesses lost revenue and customer trust, and the effects were felt for months.

NotPetya taught us a critical lesson: in our AI era, cybersecurity is not just a technical issue but a fundamental part of global business operations. It reminded everyone that preparedness and vigilance are essential to protect against the invisible but very real threats lurking in cyberspace.

These events have been startling and unsettling,

prompting us to recognize the seriousness of the risks of cyberattacks. Ted Schlein, enterprise software and security expert, once said, 'There are only two different types of companies in the world: those that have been breached and know it and those that have been breached and don't know it.' Every organization using digital systems faces some form of data security threat. With increasing digitalization, cyberattacks are on the rise. According to Steve Morgan, editor-in-chief of *Cybercrime Magazine*, cyberattacks were predicted to cause a loss of $6 trillion in 2021, which will increase by 15 per cent every year, reaching $10.5 trillion by 2025.[8] This cost includes the loss of data, loss of money, fraud, loss of business, lost productivity, theft of intellectual property, theft of personal and financial data, investigations, resumption of services, and reputational harm.

Challenges and Opportunities for Leaders of the VUCA World

How safe and secure is my system of data protection? What is my business continuity plan or disaster management plan?

Leaders of the pre-digital era used to protect physical assets using elaborate security measures. The theft of any physical asset can be detected by its absence. However, the theft of digital assets doesn't cause any deficiency as they can be copied an infinite number of times digitally. Leaders of the VUCA world need to work with advanced digital technologies, such as data analytics, to secure their digital assets—data.

Data are the new gold, and data acquisition, legal or illegal, is now crucial. The high value of data in the AI era significantly increases the risk of theft. Just as we protect our gold using multi-layer security systems (locking the house, room, almirah and iron safe), data also need to be protected using advanced cybersecurity measures. Leaders need to identify cyber risks and devise a powerful strategy to mitigate them. However safe a system may be, cyberattacks can still happen. Hackers are smart, and they know how to outsmart business leaders. While making every effort to prevent cyberattacks, leaders have to be ready with a contingency plan or company-specific business continuity plan (BCP) to deal with such attacks.

Assessment of cyber risks

The assessment of cyber risks refers to a process of identifying, analysing and evaluating the risk posed by potential cyberattacks. It ensures that the cybersecurity measures are adequate and suitable to counter the risks an organization faces. Risk identification broadly encompasses the following steps[9]:

1) *Scope of assessment*
   The assessment may be carried out for the entire organization or a part of it, like a business unit or any specific business aspect, such as payment processing or a web application.
2) *Risk identification*
   It is not possible to protect something unless you know what is to be protected and from whom. So one needs to first identify the assets—physical, digital, hardware

and network—to be protected. Then one needs to assess the possible threats to these assets.

3) *Risk analysis and evaluation*

   After identifying the risks, the next step is to assess the probability of a particular risk to the asset. This evaluation is based on factors such as the discoverability, exploitability and reproducibility of threats and vulnerabilities.

4) *Documentation*

   The identified risk and the probability of its occurrence may be recorded in a digital risk register. The risk register may be regularly reviewed and updated keeping in mind the developments taking place in cybersecurity, vulnerabilities identified and best industry practices to deal with these risks.

Business continuity plan

An organization's BCP is a document that illustrates how it will continue its business during an unexpected or unplanned disruption of services, such as a cyberattack. It is a detailed plan and includes contingencies for business processes, assets, human resources and business partners. Every aspect of the business that might be affected due to a cyberattack should be a part of a good BCP. The BCP created to deal with cyberattacks may contain plans for disaster recovery processes, data backups and replication strategies to run services from backup site locations, among other things. A good BCP is essential for an organization's resilience after cyberattacks. It is advisable to conduct mock drills to test the BCP's efficacy.

Conclusively, the leaders of the new world need to

identify cyber risks and assess the safety and security of their digital system. They are required to mitigate cyber risks, which involves establishing organizational policies ranging from employee behaviour to technical security controls. A well-drafted, tested and implementable BCP can be the saviour in case of cyberattacks.

The opportunities to succeed in the VUCA world exist in excelling in data security, winning customers' trust and out-competing others in the market. Leaders eyeing a competitive advantage need to prioritize making data privacy and protection a core part of their business. A study by Varonis suggests that only 7 per cent of people would like to use a ride-sharing service that has faced a data breach, only 14 per cent would like to use a social website after a data breach, and only 17 per cent would be willing to do business with a bank after a data breach.[10] So, while data breaches may result in a significant loss of business, robust data security can improve reputation and bring in more business.

For example, Apple laptops' competitive advantage over their rivals highlights the critical role of data security in today's business world. Customers value their advanced security features, choosing them despite the premium price for unparalleled privacy and protection.

'It is a fairly open secret that almost all systems can be hacked somehow. It is a less spoken of secret that such hacking has actually gone quite mainstream.'

—Dan Kaminsky

15

Emotional Intelligence

'Emotions are essential parts of human intelligence. Without emotional intelligence, artificial intelligence will remain incomplete.'

—Amit Ray

ON 26 SEPTEMBER 1983, THE WORLD HAD A CLOSE SHAVE WITH a potential nuclear disaster. In 1981, the Soviet Union launched Project RYaN (Raketno-Yadernoe Napadenie or nuclear missile attack).[1] The project entailed the generation of an advance alert in the case of a surprise nuclear strike from NATO member countries and the US. The system did not report any events in the first two years, but this calmness between the two superpowers of the Cold War era was rather short-lived. In 1983, the US set up a base for Pershing II ballistic missiles in West Germany. Pershing II was a mobile, intermediate-range ballistic missile that had the capability to target the Western Soviet Union in less than 10 minutes from its bases in West Germany. Each Pershing II missile could carry a single variable-yield thermonuclear warhead with an explosive force equivalent to 5–50 kilotonnes of trinitrotoluene (TNT).[2] The Soviet

Union denounced the US for disrupting the already fragile nuclear balance between them.

On 1 September 1983, a South Korean passenger jet, Korean Air Lines Flight 007, entered Soviet airspace.[3] It was shot down by the Soviet military, killing all 269 people—mostly Americans, including US Representative Larry McDonald—on board. The incident occurred when tensions between the US and Soviet Union were already at their peak during the Cold War, and the attack further deteriorated US–Soviet relations. There was intense apprehension among the Soviets that President Ronald Reagan might order the first nuclear strike on the Soviet Union at any time.

On 26 September 1983, Stanislav Petrov, a lieutenant colonel in the Soviet Air Defence Forces, was on duty at the command centre of the Soviet early warning satellites in the Serpukhov-15 bunker near Moscow. Around 15 minutes after midnight, the alarm started ringing. The system alerted twice that five intercontinental ballistic missiles of the US had been launched and were heading towards the Soviet Union. Petrov's job was to monitor expected enemy missile launches and report them to his seniors. Instead of panicking, he rightly suspected that the system was malfunctioning. Consequently, he decided to dismiss it as a false alarm. Had Petrov reported the alarm to his seniors, the Soviet military would have retaliated with a nuclear attack on the US as per war protocol. In an already politically tense situation of 1983, a retaliatory strike by the Soviet Union would have been almost certain. This could have been considered a dereliction of duty on Petrov's part, and the dutiful thing would have been to inform his superiors. Nevertheless, he believed that the US would not attack pre-emptively with just five missiles. His discernment told him that an actual attack would be big enough to destroy the Soviet Union's retaliatory capabilities. Rather than simply accepting the alarm raised by the computer system, he decided to wait for ground radar confirmation before reporting the alarm to higher-ups. The satellite radar operators did not confirm any such missile attack. However, the Soviet military treated the radar system as a support system only. Protocol clearly stated that the confirmation of a missile attack should be based on the computer system. Still, Petrov decided to ignore the alerts generated by the computer system and saved the world from nuclear annihilation. Petrov could only be sure of the correctness of his decision after 30 minutes of the alert if no missile landed on the Soviet Union. Later, it was found that the computers interpreted a reflection of sunlight on the clouds as missiles.

The story was kept under wraps for 15 years. It was too embarrassing for the Soviet military to accept that their critical security system had malfunctioned. This story came out in public only in 1998.[4]

Later in his life, Petrov gave three main reasons for considering the computer alerts false. First, when an army wages a war, it will not start with only five missiles, leaving a big enemy with the capability to retaliate. Second, there was no confirmation from the ground-based radar system, although its data might have lagged by a few minutes. Third, Petrov knew that because the system was new and had been deployed in a hurry, it may not be very accurate and reliable.

He also acknowledged in an interview with the BBC that he was the only officer in his team who had received a civilian education. He further said, 'My colleagues were all professional soldiers; they were taught to give and obey orders.'[5] If someone else had been on duty in his place, he would have reported the alarm to his seniors as per protocol.

Petrov stood out from others due to his exceptional EI, demonstrating a keen understanding of his own emotions and the ability to navigate and impact the emotions of those in his vicinity. What set Petrov apart was his intuitive grasp of the situation based on his extensive contextual knowledge. His instincts, coupled with a suspicion about the automated system's reliability, empowered him to make a rational decision in the face of uncertainty.

Emotional Intelligence vs Artificial Intelligence

It is believed that the AI era will take automation to new heights and machines will take over several jobs, even those involving cognitive abilities. This may be only partly true. EI, intuitiveness, gut feeling and the contextual understanding of situations, which are all human characteristics, cannot yet be replaced by machines. Machines are able to identify patterns in data, correlate unstructured and structured data and generate insights, but there is still no alternative to human EI. In the AI era, a lot of people will have to do what Petrov did: use EI.

It is a fact that machines equipped with AI can do certain works better than humans, thanks to the strength of machines to crunch enormous volumes of data very fast, indeed, in milliseconds. But what can humans do that machines cannot do today or in the near future? The answer is empathize, understand, motivate, inspire and interact with humans. The importance of EI in this context needs no emphasis. The AI of machines has no clue about the EI of humans.

While efforts are under way to integrate emotions into socializing robots, it is important to note that regardless of their convincing appearance, these emotions will ultimately be artificial. Socializing robots, designed to interact with humans in a social context, possess the ability to communicate, comprehend and react to human emotions, gestures and verbal cues.

In the VUCA world, when the economy is spiralling, people are facing job uncertainties and fake news is continuously blurring the truth, there will remain a need for people who possess strong EI capabilities, who are trustworthy, who can work in a hybrid team (a team of humans and machines) and who can empathize with others. The ability to manage their emotions and connect with other humans offers a clear advantage to humans where success would depend on influencing other people.

Challenges and Opportunities for Leaders of the VUCA World

How to assess my team's emotional intelligence? How to improve it?

A survey conducted by the World Economic Forum's Global Agenda Council on the Future of Software and Society predicted that EI will become one of the top skills needed by all in the future.[6] Although robots and machines can do many jobs better than humans, at the end of the day, they serve humans who, consciously or unconsciously, require human touch for their emotional needs. Even while working with machines, humans would need EI to deal with the apprehensions and anxiety caused by competition with machines. The threat of losing their jobs to machines may drive many to depression.

EI is crucial not only for leaders but also for all individual team members as it is a vital attribute necessary for effective collaboration within a team. A successful leader needs to recruit people with strong EI, assess the EI of their team and develop their EI. EI can be learned through experience and training. A leader may find appropriate training methods to enhance their team's EI. Competencies related to EI may be included as part of the continuous appraisal of the performance of employees. In addition to feedback from seniors, colleagues and juniors, a 360-degree assessment of employees may include parameters to assess their EI. Only those with excellent EI may be promoted for the responsibilities of dealing with other humans. EI will have to be made part of children's basic education as well as continuing education programmes for grownups.

Opportunities for leaders to enhance the organization's performance in the AI era lie in improving the productivity of employees through EI. A 2017 study showed that EI is highly correlated with job performance, especially the EI/EQ components of appreciating the emotions of the self and others.[7] Driven by employees' EI, there will be a positive work environment, where employees will be more productive, which will attract more talent and satisfaction for the employees, where they will be more responsive to customers. In the AI era, most of the interaction with a customer is through digital means, such as website, mobile, chatbot or interactive voice response systems. Customers' expectation of getting immediate (real-time) resolutions for their grievances is also rising. So one-to-one interaction between customers and employees of the organization, however limited it may be, would become all the more important for customer satisfaction. Employees would need a high level of EI to satisfy the demanding and difficult customers of the AI era.

Conclusively, EI is crucial for success in the VUCA world, helping employees manage anxiety, work effectively in teams, and improve customer satisfaction. Organizations should prioritize EI in recruitment, training and development to enhance productivity and performance.

'The coming era of artificial intelligence will not be the era of war, but be the era of deep compassion, non-violence, and love.'

—Amit Ray

16

Horizontal Organizational Structure

'Corporate culture matters. How management chooses to treat its people impacts everything—for better or for worse.'

—Simon Sinek

The Evolution of Assembly Lines

Before the Industrial Revolution, goods were usually made by hand by many individual experts contributing to different parts of a product. Each expert created their part of the product using their expertise and tools. Subsequently, these parts were brought together and joined to make the final product. Every product was kind of customized and made by the hands of many individuals. For example, if a bicycle was to be made, someone would make wheels, some other person would work on the frame, some would create pedals, and so on. Then these different components were assembled together to create the final product, a bicycle in this case. The process was very slow, inefficient, costly and unsuitable for mass production.

The Industrial Revolution ushered in an era of mass production, transforming the traditional manufacturing process. The automobile industry is credited with adopting the assembly line manufacturing process before any other manufacturer. Henry Ford, who founded the Ford Motor Company in 1903 in the US, was looking for ways to speed up the manufacturing of vehicles and reduce the cost so as to make the vehicles affordable for the masses. He created the Ford Model T, which could have been affordable if the production cost was reduced. In 1910, Ford set up a new manufacturing plant in Highland Park, Michigan, to increase manufacturing capacity.

He introduced the first large-scale assembly line at his Michigan plant on 1 December 1913.[1] The vehicle's chassis was pulled along an assembly line using a rope, stopping at each station for workers to add individual parts. Overall, the car manufacturing process consisted of 84 steps. A crucial factor in this process was the use of identical parts, which meant that every Model T that came off Ford's production line used identical components, such as valves, gas tanks and tyres. This approach dramatically increased the speed of assembly because the parts were mass-produced and delivered directly to the workers who were assigned to their specific assembly stations. Employee productivity improved because they performed the same tasks repeatedly. By using an assembly line, the time needed to build each vehicle reduced significantly, efficiency improved and the cost of production came down, leading to a boost in profit margins.

The assembly line is considered one of the greatest innovations of the twentieth century. It shaped the manufacturing process till the third industrial era so strongly that businesses that failed to adopt assembly lines eventually shut down. Factories equipped with robotic arms at every stage are the modern avatars of the assembly line.

Mass production driven by the assembly line also helped in creating big organizations. Unlike smaller organizations of earlier periods that were managed by a few individuals, these big organizations needed an army of personnel to manage day-to-day functions such as sales, marketing, finance, production and quality control. These organizations were typically organized vertically and had a strict hierarchical structure. Every individual was held responsible for their own duties, for which they were trained and gained experience in over time. Specialization in one task, as required for the assembly line process, was amenable to the vertical organization structure. In this type of structure, power flows from the top to the bottom. The chain of command is well defined and structured, with decisions usually taken by senior management. Decisions usually flow layer by layer from the top to the bottom, and people at the bottom have little to no autonomy. Each employee is closely monitored and supervised directly by the supervisor. The roles, responsibilities and performance parameters of each individual are clear and well defined. They are expected to work within their role and deliver the expected results. Employees' pay, perks and other incentives are linked to their productivity and often assessed through performance parameters such as productivity, sales and business generated. The vertical structure is akin to Ford's assembly line wherein each individual is required to process the work as per their defined role in the organization. Although the vertical organization structure proved its worth till the Third Industrial Revolution, it may not be suitable for the AI era. For example, in a manufacturing business, data for sales by a field unit have to flow through various levels—sales representative, sales manager, subregional manager, regional manager, etc.—before reaching the top manager. At every level, the data might be processed to sugarcoat them as incentives, for all the individuals in the chain depend upon sales figures. In the absence of autonomy, employees are deterred from sharing innovative ideas based on field experiences that higher management may not have. With multiple layers, it takes more time to gather information, respond to any problem and implement decisions.

In a vertically structured organization, multiple departments, such as marketing, operations, finance, design and development, sales, human resources, and purchase, are experts in their fields but do not always share data freely with each other. They work in silos to achieve targets for their own departments, sometimes at the cost of the organization's overall target. In a data-driven organization, there is no place for data silos. The golden record of data or master data have to be available to all departments. Whatever the limitations of a vertical organization structure may be, it has been the most successful throughout the First, Second and Third Industrial Revolutions in most organizations, including manufacturing, trading, services, government and military. Indeed, vertical structures are perhaps the only way for military organizations to succeed in their objectives.

The conventional hierarchical structure with multiple layers and departmental silos is not conducive to success in the AI era, which requires a fast, accurate and seamless flow of data across multiple departments. In the AI era, work that is repetitive and has low cognitive requirements can be performed by machines. A flat or horizontal organizational structure is more suitable for modern organizations (Figure 16.1). In this kind of structure, there are very few layers of management and usually a short chain of command. Employees have the freedom to share information/data with the top management, make decisions, propose innovative ideas and discuss their views freely. Employees from different departments are encouraged to share information and work together as a cohesive team. With the engagement and inclusion of every level of employee in the development of the organization, employees feel motivated and contribute more.

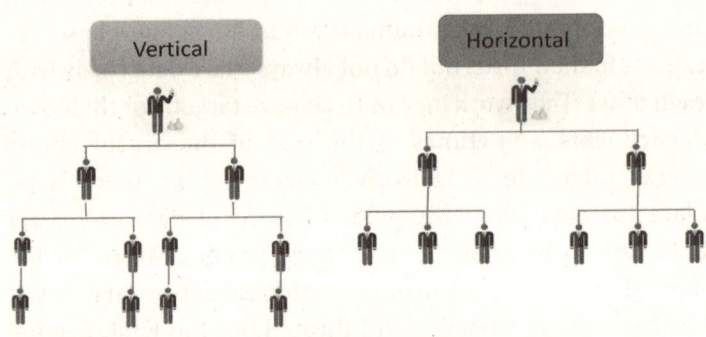

Figure 16.1: Vertical vs Horizontal Organizational Structure

An article, 'Building the AI-Powered Organization- Technology Isn't the Biggest Challenge. Culture Is', has identified the following three shifts required by companies to scale up the adoption of AI in their business processes[2]:

- From siloed work to interdisciplinary collaboration
- From experience-based, leader-driven decision-making to data-driven decision-making at the frontline
- From rigid and risk-averse to agile, experimental and adaptable

In the AI era, the above shifts cannot be made without replacing a vertical organizational structure with a horizontal one. The middle layers (managers) of the organization can be replaced with business intelligence tools that are capable of monitoring and managing the working of lower layers more efficiently and without human biases. Data need to flow seamlessly through different layers across departments. Today, businesses have data warehouses (DWs) or data lakes (DLs) where all the data generated by the organization are pooled. Users can access the required data from the DW/DL as per their needs.

The transformation from a vertical to a horizontal organizational structure is also required to attract new generations to work for the organization. Millennials born between 1980 and 2000 prefer a flatter and more flexible organizational structure over a traditional rigid organizational structure. According to a survey report titled 'Millennials at Work'[3]:

> Millennials tend to be uncomfortable with rigid corporate structures and turned off by information silos. They expect rapid progression, a varied and interesting career and constant feedback. In other words, millennials want a management style and corporate culture that is markedly different from

anything that has gone before—one that meets their needs.

Challenges and Opportunities for Leaders of the VUCA World

How to re-engineer the organizational structure in tune with the AI era?

Leaders of the AI era need to restructure organizations horizontally, perhaps by removing middle layers and breaking silos by pooling data generated across departments. This may be easier for a new organization than for legacy ones. There is no one-size-fits-all solution for different types of organizations. Every organization will have to find its own path to shift from a vertical to horizontal structure or any combination of the two (hybrid structure). This process has to be gradual but steady. Organizations need to re-evaluate numerous established practices and remove intermediate hierarchical layers to facilitate the adoption of a horizontal structure. This may be a major culture shock for employees who are accustomed to a particular hierarchical structure. Change management through the collaborative involvement of employees, empowerment of employees and effective communication would facilitate such a transformation. New employees may be recruited, considering the changing nature of the organizational structure. So, instead of hiring the most qualified person for a specific task, leaders need to place more emphasis on cultural fit and adaptability, driving home the fact that the employee's role will transform along with the implementation of AI. Soft skills, such as communication skills, critical thinking, creativity, EI and teamwork, will be more important than technical skills. Leaders need to move away from top-down structures, move towards multidisciplinary teams and redesign their organizations to be team-centric. As AI capabilities improve, leaders will have to decide where to use humans, which tasks can be best performed by machines and which can be jointly done by both. The organizational structure needs to be developed according to the varied roles of humans and machines, and a flat organization seems to be the way forward.

The future lies in leveraging the benefits of a horizontal structure, which may help reduce manpower; encourage innovation; improve productivity, the seamless flow of data, data-driven decision-making and employee satisfaction; and be more responsive to customers.

'If you get the culture right, most of the other stuff will just take care of itself.'

–Tony Hsieh

17

The Future of Work: Work 5.0

'People are more productive working at home than people would have expected. Some people thought that everything was just going to fall apart, and it hasn't.'

—Mark Zuckerberg

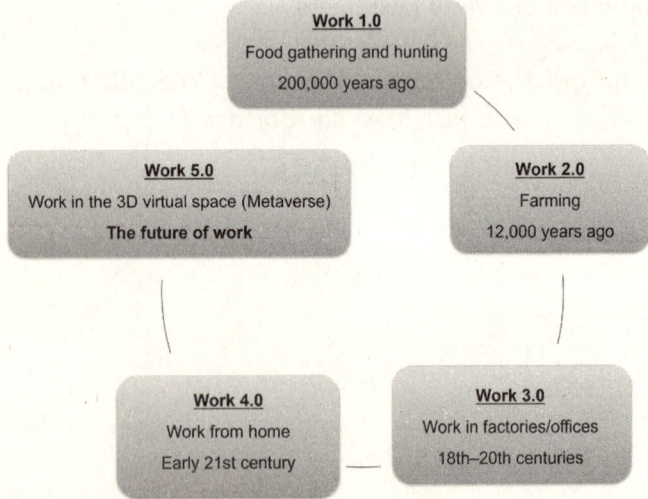

Figure 17.1: Evolution of work

The history of work can be traced back to around 200,000 years ago to the origin of our species. Here, the word 'work' is being used in the context of earning a livelihood. Early humans were foragers who gathered and hunted food, and their lives involved continuous movement in search of food. *Work 1.0*, which involved food gathering and hunting, was the first form of job humans started with.

Around 12,000 years ago, humans learned to cultivate food, thereby ushering in an agricultural revolution. They started settling in groups near their farmland and domesticating animals for their daily needs; eventually, an entire village would come into being. Home-based industries like pottery, weaving and handicrafts started growing to meet the needs of the village dwellers. *Work at home* for these home-based businesses and *work near home* for farming in fields near settlements were the primary forms of *Work 2.0*, which continued for ages.

The Industrial Revolution started with the invention of the industrial steam engine in 1776. This was followed by the rapid expansion of factories—for the mass production of goods—railways, road vehicles, aeroplanes, and so on. The latter half of the nineteenth century witnessed an era of innovations and technological advancements, which helped the emergence of new energy sources, namely, electricity, gas and oil. The share of the service sector in the economy started increasing, and more people started working in banks, trading firms, financial institutions and other service organizations. Working in factories/offices (Work 3.0), which started with the Industrial Revolution, was the new normal for urban life until recently.

The twenty-first century brought success stories of AI,

big data, IoT and the virtualization of physical space. The lightning speed of communication driven by 4G/5G mobile communication technology allowed netizens to work from anywhere. *Work from home (WFH) (Work 4.0)* started to look like a viable option. According to the American Community Survey 2017 (even before the COVID-19 pandemic), 5.2 per cent of total workers or 8 million people in the US worked from home in 2017.[1]

The year 2020 witnessed the start of the COVID-19 era and soon turned into a watershed moment for mankind. On 30 January 2020, the WHO announced COVID-19 to be a public health emergency and declared it a pandemic on 11 March 2020. By early April 2020, half of the world's population was advised to stay at home by their governments to control the spread of the deadly virus. During the lockdown, many firms in the service sector smoothly transitioned to a WFH model, ensuring business continuity for clients without compromising on quality or productivity. The common belief that WFH is a short-term phenomenon has not turned out to be true. Despite large-scale vaccination, major IT giants are continuing with WFH completely or partly (employees come to the office once or twice a week). Workers also prefer working from remote locations to avoid the hassle of commuting and wasting precious time. In fact, the flexibility to work from remote locations has become an incentive for employees during recruitment. Although many industries like manufacturing, transportation, hospitality and healthcare cannot, by their nature, accept WFH at this stage, in the future, robots are likely to replace humans in many of these sectors and humans will be able to control robots while sitting at home.

Communication in the WFH model in its present form is limited due to the absence of body language, which is an integral part of any social interaction. As social animals, humans adopt body language much before acquiring linguistic skills to express themselves. A major part of human communication is indeed non-verbal. Albert Mehrabian, a renowned body language researcher, found that in face-to-face communication, 55 per cent is non-verbal, 38 per cent is vocal and only 7 per cent is conveyed through words.[2] However, WFH in a 2D space is devoid of this essential mode of human expression.

WFH has already found a new avatar *(Work 5.0)* in the metaverse whereby work will shift to a 3D virtual space. The metaverse concept offers the potential to establish a digital realm that is fully immersive, interactive and collaborative. This innovative world integrates various technologies, including mixed reality (MR), such as augmented reality (AR) and virtual reality (VR), as well as 3D holographic avatars, IoT and digital twins. In the virtual space of the metaverse, users are represented by avatars. An avatar plays the role of the user in the shared virtual space of the metaverse. So, in the metaverse, the avatars of humans will be able to interact in a 3D virtual space the way we do in a physical space today. These avatars use verbal as well as non-verbal modes of communication to express themselves. The metaverse creates an immersive virtual workplace wherein 3D avatars of people can interact and work together as in the real world. For remote workers, the immersive experience could dramatically improve user experience and their efficiency. This is the biggest advantage of working in the metaverse.

Further, some tasks and business problems would require a visual interface that is not easy to create in the real world. For example, an architect may like to present the model of a building in a 3D space or an engineer may like to present a new car model in a 3D space. The metaverse might make it possible to visualize multiple layers of an object in a 3D virtual space. In the metaverse, one can even enter different rooms in the virtual model of a building.

The metaverse offers a virtual space where one can simulate anything from the real world and the specifications can be replicated via digital twin technology. Simulation facilitates smarter problem-solving in several industries like architecture, construction, automobiles, airlines, healthcare and life sciences. Another advantage of working in the metaverse would be the unlimited availability of space or features one may like to use. One can use multiple tools for business intelligence, visualization and modelling as a service from numerous service providers.

As with any other technology, the introduction of the metaverse has its challenges in terms of infrastructure and data security. To work in the metaverse, one requires a set of full-body equipment and sensors, sophisticated headsets and powerful cloud connectivity on 5G mobile communication. The enabling infrastructure for the metaverse might take several years to develop. The inconvenience of putting on full-body gear would be another challenge impacting the adoption of the metaverse as a workplace in the near future. Further, there are concerns around security because the metaverse would capture personal data to be able to provide an intuitive and immersive experience. Certainly, tech companies that are investing billions in metaverse technologies will produce secure and user-friendly gadgets in due course.

Over the last 200,000 years, Work 1.0, which entailed food gathering and hunting, evolved into Work 2.0 (working in fields/at home) and Work 3.0 (working in factories/offices) and has now transformed into Work 4.0 (working from home). The metaverse has thrown open the next level of possibilities by creating a virtual 3D workspace with an immersive experience. The future of work—Work 5.0—lies in working in immersive virtual spaces that provide a 'real-world' experience.

Figure 17.2[3]: Evolution of work

Challenges and Opportunities for Leaders of the VUCA World

How to adopt work-from-anywhere in the organization?

In today's AI era where remote work has become the norm

rather than the exception, leaders need to find innovative ways to adopt work-from-anywhere and constructively engage employees in hybrid work conditions. This is especially important as companies are increasingly embracing remote work policies to meet the demands of the changing workforce and evolving business landscape.

The first critical step in creating a successful work-from-anywhere programme is developing a work-from-anywhere policy (WfAP) for employees. A comprehensive policy makes remote working a win–win for employers and employees by clearly communicating expectations, responsibilities and conduct. Defining who is eligible and ineligible for remote work and outlining legal liabilities in the event of an injury at the place of work (anywhere) reduces misunderstandings or conflicts between employees and managers about what is expected when working from anywhere.

Another important consideration when creating a WfAP is cybersecurity. Remote employees need to access the company's IT system through the internet, which increases the risk of cyberattacks. As a result, clear protocol for accessing IT systems using secured VPNs as well as dos and don'ts may be required to minimize the risk of cyberattacks.

To make work from anywhere truly effective, leaders will need to provide the right tools for collaboration and communication. In addition to traditional communication methods such as email, phone and instant messaging, leaders may consider adopting the metaverse to build virtual offices and improve the effectiveness of remote working. The metaverse offers an immersive virtual world where employees can interact with one another as if they were in a physical office, regardless of their location.

Working from anywhere has significant benefits. For instance, employees can enjoy a better work–life balance, which can lead to higher job satisfaction, less burnout and improved mental health. Additionally, WfAPs can help attract new talent and retain existing employees by offering greater flexibility and reducing the cost of maintaining a physical office.

Another advantage of working from anywhere is that it offers a unique opportunity to engage talent from anywhere around the world. With a global talent pool, businesses can leverage the skills of people from different cultures and backgrounds, leading to a diverse and innovative workforce.

Ultimately, leaders who successfully embrace work from anywhere will be better positioned to compete in the global economy of the twenty-first century.

'Do you want to access talent everywhere, or just in specific markets? If the answer is everywhere, you need to be at least open to the possibility of remote work.'

—Katie Burke

18

Human Resource Management

'One machine can do the work of fifty ordinary men. No machine can do the work of one extraordinary man.'

—Elbert Hubbard

Knocker upper in England[1]

Knocker Upper

During the First Industrial Revolution, machine-made goods replaced hand-made ones. Steam engines become ubiquitous in factories. Humans became the operators of these machines. Productivity increased immensely. Machines were able to work round the clock and produce more, justifying their capital cost. Human operators needed to work in shifts to keep these machines functional 24×7. The shift started early in the morning. Today, it may sound unbelievable, but at that time, how to wake people up early in the morning was a major challenge.

Mechanical alarm clocks used to be quite expensive and were unreliable. Consequently, a new profession was founded called knocker upper. Knocker uppers would wake people up early in the morning so that they could reach the factories in time for the morning shift.

Typically, a knocker upper would wake up around 3 a.m. and go around the place to wake people up at the requested time. A knocker upper would serve 50–100 clients. They used bamboo sticks to knock on windows on the upper floors. The knocker upper would receive around one shilling per week from a client. The fee often depended upon the time and distance of the client's house. Waking up at early hours such as 4 a.m. was more expensive than the later hours between 5 a.m. and 6 a.m. If a knocker upper failed to wake up their client, the client would be late for work and might lose their job. The knocker upper would not leave a client's window without ensuring that they had been woken. So, knocker uppers were widely respected and their fees was paid on time.

Many people were engaged in this job, especially in larger industrial towns such as Manchester. Generally, elder men and women would perform this job, but sometimes, police constables also performed this job to augment their earnings.

With the advent of reliable and affordable alarm clocks in the 1950s, the knocker upper profession slowly died out by the 1970s.

Knocker upper is just one example of jobs that were replaced by technology. In a bygone era, streetlamp lighters, lift operators, telephone operators and cashiers similarly succumbed to automation's relentless march. Streetlamp lighters, once responsible for illuminating city streets, have been replaced by automated lighting systems. Lift operators, who manually managed elevator operations, became obsolete with the advent of self-service mechanisms. Telephone operators, who manually connected calls, were rendered unnecessary with the advent of automated switchboards. Likewise, cashiers, whose roles involved manual transaction processing, found their positions transformed by self-checkout systems. The inexorable progress of technology has reshaped the employment landscape, making certain traditional roles relics of the past.

After the First Industrial Revolution, many jobs were no more needed thanks to the invention of machines. The invention of the steam engine way back in the seventeenth century ushered in an era of machines replacing the muscle power of human beings. The competition was between the muscle power of humans and machines. Of course, machines proved to be more powerful. However, in the second machine age, led by AI, the competition is between human brain power and machine intelligence, and it is apparent that intelligent machines have the potential to replace humans in many areas of brain power. AI is already helping business leaders automate business processes, gain insights through advanced data analytics—predictive and post-event—and engage with customers and employees with NLP chatbots. This transformation signifies the ongoing evolution of the workforce, whereby new technology reshapes employment opportunities and renders certain roles redundant.

Digitalization is posing many new challenges regarding human resource management for organizations in terms of building a culture of continuous learning, hybrid working (work from remote locations, freelancing and work–life balance), working with machines and dealing with young and old generations.

Continuous Learning Programmes

In the AI era, leaders must consistently enhance employee skills to remain relevant. Traditionally, individuals would acquire a single skill or specialize in areas like engineering, finance or medicine, sustaining their careers with gradual experiential learning. However, this gradual learning approach is unsuitable in the face of AI/ML-driven digitalization, which not only provides diverse opportunities but also disrupts conventional job markets. The current landscape demands a shift away from the traditional model, emphasizing continuous skill upgradation to align with the dynamic challenges presented by technological advancements, particularly in the realms of AI and ML.

New jobs are being created and older ones are being

taken away. Some examples of new jobs are data scientists, ML engineers, cybersecurity experts, AI ethics specialists and AI product manager, and the most recent one is prompt engineering. Data scientists analyse complex data to extract insights for data-driven decision making, ML engineers are pivotal in developing adaptive algorithms, AI ethics specialists ensure whether ethical practices are being followed while developing AI models, and AI/cybersecurity researchers bolster digital security. AI product managers oversee AI product life cycles, reflecting the evolving landscape. Concurrently, generative AI, exemplified by models like GPT-4, has birthed a new field—prompt engineering. This involves crafting precise instructions or prompts to guide generative models. Recognized by engineers and users alike, prompt engineering requires understanding model nuances and strategic phrasing for applications like creative writing and problem-solving. This emerging field enables effective communication with sophisticated AI models, thereby unlocking possibilities across diverse domains, including creative writing, programming and content generation.

The confluence of technological progress and shifting job roles vividly illustrates the transformative influence of AI/ML on industries and employment. Consequently, individuals in the AI era are compelled to engage in frequent skill acquisition through programmes dedicated to skill upgradation. It is often said that to stay relevant in this digital landscape, individuals need to acquire new skills approximately every 10 years. Figure 18.1 illustrates the contrast between conventional learning curves and the accelerated learning curve demanded by the AI era, which underscores the urgency for continuous skill development in response to the rapid evolution of technology.

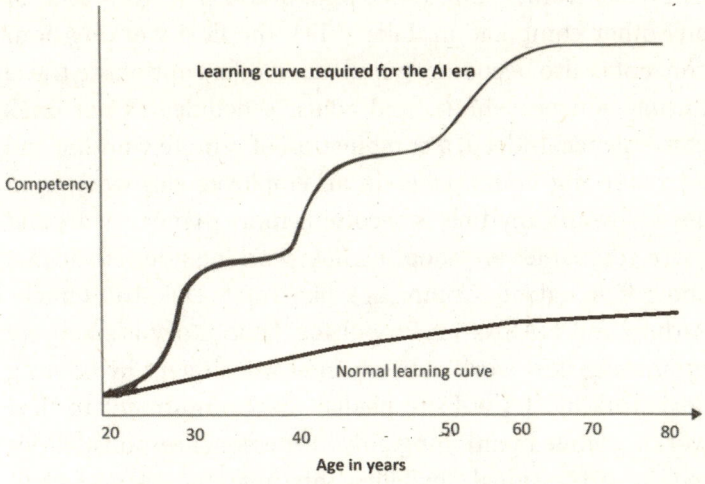

Figure 18.1: Learning curve for the AI era

Hybrid and Flexi Working

As discussed in the previous chapter, a major change being witnessed in human resource management is the rising aspiration of next-gen employees to work from anywhere with flexible working hours. Today, remote working is generally preferred by employees and employers for its benefits, inter alia, freedom from commuting and savings from foregoing office space, respectively. A flexible working schedule allows an employee to work at times that differ from the usual office work schedule. Normal working hours in an office may be from 9 a.m. to 6 p.m., but a flexible schedule allows the employee to work any time as per one's convenience, say, from 12 p.m. to 9 p.m., 7 a.m. to 4 p.m., in breaks from 7 a.m. to 12 p.m. and 4 p.m. to 8 p.m. or any other combination. Like WFH, the flexi-working-hour concept is also becoming popular as it offers options to travel during non-peak hours and adjust schedules as per one's convenience. Indeed, a combination of remote working and flexi working hours, wherein an employee can work from anywhere and anytime, is becoming more popular. More and more companies are adopting flexi working hours to attract and retain talent. Companies like Intel, Deloitte, Oracle, Airbnb and NASA's Jet Propulsion Laboratory are actively promoting flexi work options. Intel woos talent by offering flexi working. Its website pledges its commitment to flexi working while mentioning, 'If your personal responsibilities require professional flexibility, Intel may be the perfect fit for you. We offer creative approaches to help you meet your commitments in life. From compressed workweeks, flexitime, and alternate start times to telecommuting and part-time and job share positions, each business unit has a range of options for you to explore.'[2]

Gig Economy (Freelancing)

The term freelancer or freelance worker refers to an individual who is self-employed and does not have a long-term commitment to a specific employer. The system of permanent jobs is increasingly being replaced by temporary engagement for specific projects/work for a limited duration. We are entering an era of the free market system, also called the gig economy, in which temporary positions are common and organizations sign contracts with independent workers for short-term engagements. By definition, a gig means a project, task or assignment for which a person is hired on demand for the duration of the project. A McKinsey Global Institute report estimated that 20–30 per cent of the working-age population or about 162 million individuals in the US and EU-15 engage in independent work.[3] Contrary to conventional belief, most independent workers opt for freelancing out of preference rather than necessity, and they report being highly satisfied with their work lives. This unprecedented growth in freelancing was beyond imagination a few years ago.

The motivations behind the preference for freelancing are numerous. Most importantly, in this AI era, work can be done from anywhere, any time. The location, time and job are decoupled because a person need not be at the workplace at a specific time to render their responsibilities. Thus, freelancers can select locations independent of multiple temporary works around the world. Employers can also select the best workers suited for the project from a large pool of available freelancers specialized in the desired work without much training or a long-term commitment. The gig economy is also perceived to provide better work–life balance to freelancers, thanks to the flexibility offered by freelancing jobs.

In response to the market volatility brought about by the COVID-19 pandemic, several companies have transitioned to an agile workforce comprising independent workers. Additionally, pandemic-related layoffs and the rising cost of living have prompted more workers to opt for independent work arrangements. This shift may be attributed to the challenge of securing permanent employment or to the inadequate salary earned from primary employment.

Work-Life Balance

In the AI era, employees remain connected to work/their workplace 24 hours a day and 7 days a week through electronic devices. Although digitalization offers a lot of flexibility in working hours, 24×7 connectivity may challenge work–life balance. This may increase mental stress, put constant pressure and lower employee motivation and productivity. It may also cause emotional and psychological disturbance to employees. Leaders of the AI era will have to find ways to maintain work–life balance for employees, including frequent holidays, long weekends and no email/messages during non-working hours. Leaders need to create a work culture that empowers and motivates employees to maintain a healthy work–life balance. By discarding outdated management practices and adopting a new perspective, we can fully reap the advantages of digitalization and develop robust and sustainable workplaces. These work environments should prioritize employee enjoyment, engagement and overall happiness. By doing so, a leader can distinguish themself as the best employer in the AI era and woo talented employees to join the organization.

Work with Machines

'This is not a race against the machines.
If we race against them, we lose. This is a race with machines. You'll be paid in the future based on how well

> *you work with robots. Ninety percent of your coworkers will be unseen machines.'*
>
> —Kevin Kelly

While the notion of seamlessly integrating humans with intelligent machines might seem utopian, historical shifts demonstrate its plausibility. In the early nineteenth century, 70 per cent of American workers toiled in agriculture. Gradually, automation replaced nearly all these jobs and gave rise to millions in the manufacturing and service sectors. The ongoing Fourth Industrial Revolution is poised for a similar paradigm shift. Automation will likely optimize tasks previously handled by humans, hence posing a challenge for leaders to not only replace human roles with machines but also cultivate in employees the skills needed for collaborative work with intelligent technologies. History suggests that despite initial disruptions, these transitions can lead to the creation of new, diversified job opportunities, emphasizing the importance of proactively preparing the workforce for the evolving dynamics of man–machine collaboration in the AI era.

Challenges and Opportunities for Leaders of the VUCA World

How to keep my workforce relevant in the AI era? What new skills/training should be imparted?

Leaders will have to create an enabling environment wherein man and machine can work side by side, compensate for the other's weaknesses and complement the other's strengths. To keep pace with technology, leaders would need to cultivate in employees a culture of lifelong learning. They will have to offer tools and support to ensure the employees update their skills in line with contemporary and upcoming technologies. Workers in the gig economy expect flexibility and freedom. Leaders will have to explore ways to enable work from a remote location and offer work–life balance. They would have to focus on three main functions to transform their work culture in tandem with the AI era:

- Employ people with digital skills, including data science; data-based management and decision-making; agility; and data orientation.
- Develop a culture conducive for employees to innovate, be creative and think out of the box. It needs to be appreciated that failures are part of innovation, but learning from failures is valuable for successful innovations.
- Employees should be trained and rewarded for moving away from traditional practices and displaying novelty in their approach.

The traditional workplace will have to be transformed into a modern one that embraces the reality of digital collaboration, solutions and integration as the way of the future. Office spaces may be redesigned to pave the way for technologies supporting automation, digital workspaces and hybrid work.

Leaders are required to develop a culture of innovation, creativity, collaboration and continuous learning using digital means. The synergy between the strengths of humans and machines may take organizations to new heights, but an enabling environment has to be developed by leaders. The key to success in the AI era lies in training employees in the latest technologies, equipping them with the support required to perform their duties and keeping them motivated. Human resource will remain the most valuable resource even in the AI era; however, the role may undergo a change from a worker to an innovator, thought leader and collaborator.

'The competition to hire the best will increase in the years ahead. Companies that give extra flexibility to their employees will have the edge in this area.'

—Bill Gates

19

Predictive Analytics and Demand Forecasting

'Information is the oil of the 21st century, and analytics is the combustion engine.'

—Peter Sondergaard

IN THE NINETEENTH CENTURY, THE SPREAD OF THE CHOLERA epidemic killed thousands of people worldwide. It is now fully established that cholera, a bacterial disease, spreads through contaminated water. At that time, however, the common belief was that cholera was caused by breathing poisonous air. John Snow, a British doctor, was of the view that cholera was a waterborne disease and spread by consuming contaminated water. He published a book titled *On the Mode of Communication of Cholera* in 1849 in support of his theory.[1] However, his theory did not get much attention from the medical fraternity until 1854.

In nineteenth-century Britain, most people used town wells and handpumps as a source of drinking water. The untreated sewerage from homes was dumped into the Thames river or open pits called cesspools.

In August 1854, cholera spread in the Broad Street area of Soho, a suburb of London. In a few days, hundreds died of cholera in the region. People began fleeing the city. Dr Snow lived in a nearby area. He started collecting data and interviewing victims' families. Snow found that a handpump on Broad Street may be the source of contaminated water. He collected the names and addresses of the first 83 victims who died in the first week of the first reported case. By interviewing the victims' families, he learned that most of them sourced their water from the same handpump. On 6 September 1854, Snow, in a meeting with the local authorities, claimed that contaminated water from the handpump was responsible for the cholera outbreak and suggested that the pump handle be removed. The local authorities, although unconvinced, agreed to remove the handle as a precaution. The epidemic began to subside quickly and was controlled within days.

Further, an investigation of 197 victims by Snow revealed that most of them lived within walking distance of the pump. He also observed that a nearby workhouse and brewery (Lion Brewery) were least affected by the epidemic as they had their independent source of water. He studied the data of people living near other handpumps and found that they were also the least impacted by the epidemic. He developed a spot map of the area near the pump and marked the victims' homes. Cholera cases are highlighted in black, showing the clusters of cases (indicated by stacked rectangles). The location of the pump, the workhouse and the brewery are encircled in the spot map. The map clearly showed the clustering of victims around the handpump.

However, the reason for the contamination of the

handpump water was still unknown. After some days, the handpump was made operational without any further incident. Dr Snow's theory that cholera was caused by contaminated water was still in question. However, after some months, an associate of Dr Snow found records of the death of an infant due to cholera at the beginning of the outbreak.[2] She was perhaps the first cholera case reported in that area. The infant's mother revealed that she dumped a pail of the infant's faeces into a cesspool in front of their house, which was adjacent to the water pump. The cesspool, which was just three feet from the well, was found to be leaking due to decayed walls. With these findings, it could be conclusively proved that cholera spread through contaminated water.

Predictive Analytics and Demand Forecasting 187

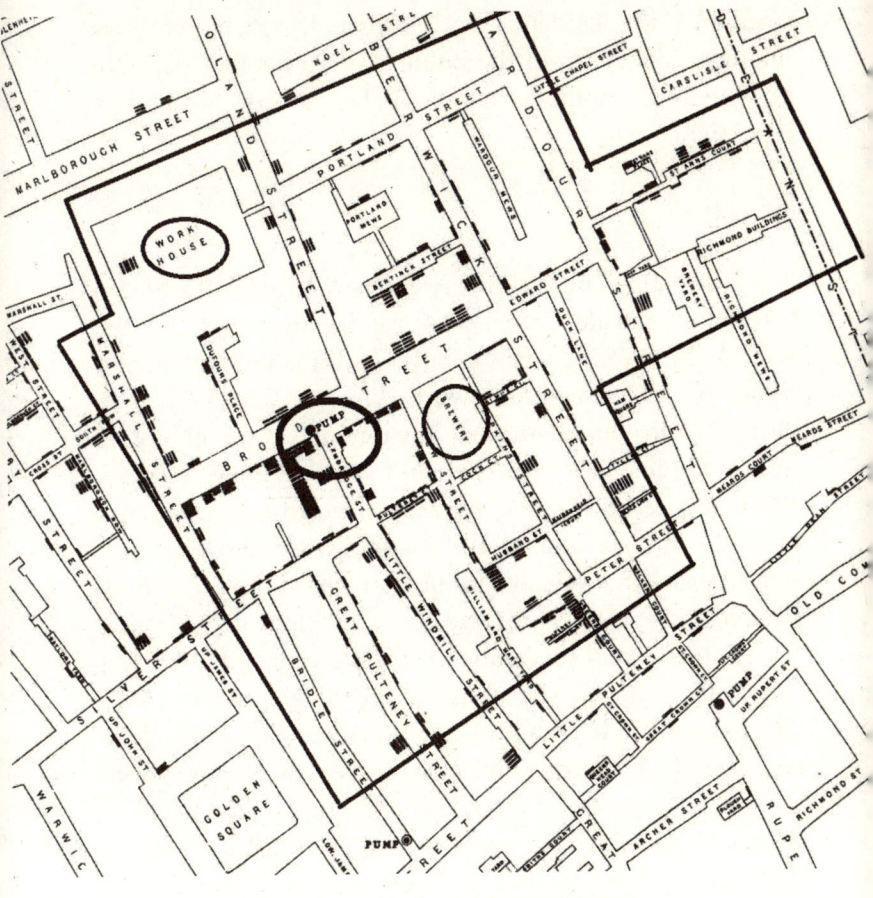

Spot map made by Dr John Snow, 1854[3]

Dr Snow had to manually collect and analyse the volumes of data and addresses of victims, interview hundreds of residents and develop a spot map to prove his theory. He is considered the father of epidemiology for this groundbreaking research. He spent several months to determine the cause of the spread of the epidemic and ultimately reach definitive findings. Indeed, from the publication of his first paper in 1849 to 1854, thousands of people had already succumbed to cholera.

COVID-19

The years 2020 and 2021 were eclipsed by COVID-19. Do you know, outside China, who was the first to detect the spread of COVID-19 in Wuhan? No, it was not any human being. An AI platform known as BlueDot was the first to detect a cluster of unusual pneumonia cases emerging near a vibrant market in Wuhan, China.[4] With a keen eye, BlueDot sifted through a myriad of foreign-language news reports, intricate animal and plant disease networks and official proclamations. It skilfully unravelled the impending pandemic's trajectory, foreseeing its ominous expansion.

At the heart of BlueDot's remarkable capabilities lies the symbiotic fusion of AI and big data. Through the art of NLP and finesse of ML, BlueDot embarked on a quest to glean and crunch data from multiple sources. Statements from authoritative public health organizations, the vast realm of digital media, intricate tapestry of global airline ticketing data, labyrinthine reports on livestock health and mosaic of population demographics all came under BlueDot's discerning gaze.

BlueDot's algorithm continuously collects data from every corner of the globe. This vast amount of information is processed every 15 minutes, day and night. It stood as a testament to the power of technology, tirelessly parsing and interpreting the evolving landscape of information. The platform emerged as an omnipresent sentinel, observing, analysing and providing invaluable insights into the ever-shifting tapestry of our world.

BlueDot flagged it on 30 December 2019, nine days before the WHO released its first alert on the emergence of a novel coronavirus. BlueDot deployed AI to track, locate and conceptualize infectious disease spread.

In addition to detecting the origin of an epidemic/pandemic, BlueDot was able to accurately predict how the disease would spread to other parts of the world. BlueDot was also able to identify the cities closely connected with Wuhan using global airline ticketing data. BlueDot correctly predicted these cities as Bangkok, Hong Kong, Tokyo, Taipei, Phuket, Seoul and Singapore.

Governments across the world used IT tools to predict the spread of COVID-19. The Indian government launched Aarogya Setu to notify users if they had crossed paths with someone who tested positive. The mobile app enabled Bluetooth-based contact tracing, the mapping of likely hotspots and dissemination of relevant information about COVID-19.

Cholera vs COVID-19: Use of Predictive Analytics

A comparison of the two cases shows how technology has changed the way epidemics/pandemics are tracked, traced and controlled. There was a time when the collection and diagnostic analysis of a small volume of data to find the reason for the spread of an epidemic in a city used to take months if not years. During that time, the disease would spread unabated. Today, AI-enabled predictive analytics tools are capable of scouring large volumes of data from across the world in minutes, accurately finding the origin point of the diseases and predicting the spread of diseases. Predictive analytics tools are proving to be game changers in many fields, such as health, manufacturing, services, finance and supply chain. Let us discuss predictive analytics further.

Predictive Analytics

IBM defines predictive analytics as follows: '[...] a branch of advanced analytics that makes predictions about future outcomes using historical data combined with statistical modelling, data mining techniques and machine learning. Companies employ predictive analytics to find patterns in this data to identify risks and opportunities. Predictive analytics is often associated with big data and data science.'[5]

These days, every organization is sitting on piles of data generated from customers, operations and maintenance. These data can be used to predict the future with the help of predictive analytics. Forecasting can enable leaders to make better decisions and formulate data-driven strategies. Some of the use cases of predictive analytics are as follows:

- **Demand forecasting:** Organizations can forecast the demand for products based on historical sales and other contributing factors affecting demand (weather, trends, social media, etc.) and optimize their supply chain to make it efficient. For example, Amazon uses big data to predict what goods customers are likely to buy, when they will buy them and where they will need the things. Then the products are transported from the supplier to a nearby fulfilment centre (warehouse) to be ready for transit when the customer demands them. This is how Amazon is able to meet the customer's demand within a minimum time and become the most preferred e-commerce website. Similarly, a mineral water company can forecast demand by analysing seasonal trends, weather patterns and heatwave forecasts. Increased temperatures and summer months typically drive higher demand, whereas cooler seasons may reduce it. Incorporating weather forecasts into inventory and production planning allows the company to optimize supply and efficiently meet customer needs.

- **Predictive maintenance:** AI/ML tools are used to predict equipment failure based on the historical data of similar failures. Predictive analytics helps organizations take timely action and prevent failures, thus improving the reliability and availability of assets and saving the cost incurred on frequent periodic preventive maintenance. For example, ThyssenKrupp, a major elevator manufacturer in the world, uses an IoT-based MAX predictive maintenance solution. MAX, a cutting-edge system, gathers real-time data from the connected elevators, which is then sent to the cloud.[6] Through advanced algorithms, it calculates the remaining lifetime of key components, accurately determining maintenance needs. Elevator efficiency and reliability reach new heights with MAX's innovative approach.
- **Disease prediction:** The data collected from

wearables (smartwatches, mobile phones, etc.) are being used to predict the onset of diseases.
- **Risk modelling:** Insurance companies are using predictive analytics to do risk assessments and evaluate the premiums required for different insurance products. Risk modelling also helps in formulating risk management strategies and minimizing the impact of risks.
- **Fraud detection:** Empowering proactive defence and safeguarding against deception, a predictive analytics application diligently scrutinizes the system's anomalies. It possesses an astute ability to identify peculiar behaviours and patterns, thus swiftly uncovering threats and thwarting fraudulent activities with precision and efficiency. Banks, insurance companies and other financial institutions now use predictive analytics to prevent fraud.

Challenges and Opportunities for Leaders of the VUCA World

How to use predictive analytics for demand forecasting and asset management in my business?

The use of AI and ML has revolutionized the way businesses operate. With their ability to process vast amounts of data and make predictions based on those data, these technologies have become invaluable for companies looking to improve efficiency, reduce costs and gain a competitive edge in their respective markets.

Predictive analytics enhances demand forecasting,

enabling efficient inventory and production planning. It optimizes asset maintenance by predicting equipment failures, reducing downtime and costs. Additionally, it detects fraud through pattern analysis, safeguarding businesses in sectors like banking and finance.

To fully leverage the power of predictive analytics, businesses need to have the right tools and technologies. This may include data analytics software, ML algorithms and other tools that can help process and analyse large datasets. Additionally, businesses need to clearly understand the data they are collecting and how they can be used to improve their operations.

Leaders in the AI era need to be aware of the potential benefits of predictive analytics and demand forecasting. By adopting these technologies early on, businesses can gain a significant competitive advantage and stay ahead of the curve. However, it is important to adopt these technologies in a strategic and deliberate manner, ensuring that the right tools and technologies are in place and that employees are properly trained to use them effectively.

Ultimately, businesses that are able to effectively leverage the power of predictive analytics and demand forecasting will thrive in the AI era. By using data-driven insights to make informed decisions, these businesses will be able to stay ahead of the competition, improve their operational efficiency and achieve long-term success.

The traditional view that technology should first be established and proven and only then be adopted is not meant for the AI era. Early adopters of technology may gain so much ground within a short time that late adopters would never be able to catch up and be left behind. Truly speaking, business leaders can ill afford to miss the opportunities made available by predictive analytics and demand forecasting.

'Data analytics is the future, and the future is NOW! Every mouse click, keyboard button press, swipe or tap is used to shape business decisions. Everything is about data these days. Data is information, and information is power.'

—Radi

20

Responsible AI

'Success in creating AI would be the biggest event in human history. Unfortunately, it might also be the last, unless we learn how to avoid the risks.'

—Stephen Hawking

CHINA'S STATE COUNCIL RELEASED DIRECTIVES IN 2014 THAT outlined the implementation of a social credit system (SCS) by 2020. As a part of this system, each adult is assigned a credit code alongside their government-issued identity card. The primary objectives are to encourage positive economic and ethical conduct. The proposed criteria for evaluating citizens and assigning them a numerical rating, known as social credit, encompassed factors like financial status, criminal history and online interactions on social media platforms. The guidelines state[1]:

> It is supported by the lawful application of credit information and a credit services system, its inherent requirements are establishing the idea of a sincerity culture, and carrying forward sincerity and traditional virtues, it uses encouragement to keep trust and constraints against breaking trust as incentive

mechanisms, and its objective is raising the honest mentality and credit levels of the entire society.

China's SCS for its citizens is fuelled by advancements in AI, big data and IoT. The SCS is a step towards creating a credit score-based society. The system monitors the behaviour of China's large population and rates them as per their credit score. China uses a complex algorithm to assign credit scores to everyone. The methodology used to calculate the social score is not available in the public domain for obvious reasons, but some factors that may adversely impact credit score include rash driving, traffic violation, misbehaving on a train, throwing garbage on the street, smoking in non-smoking zones, buying too many video games and posting false information online. Citizens with poor credit scores have to face penalties such as non-availability of loans, no admissions to good educational institutes, being ineligible for certain jobs and no tickets to travel in trains/airplanes. There is no single SCS across China. Different cities have their own rating systems that work differently. Typically, in the beginning, certain points (say, 1000 points) are credited to a citizen's SCS account. City authorities debit these points for bad behaviours and credit points for good behaviours. CCTV cameras equipped with facial recognition capabilities have been installed across cities to continuously monitor the behaviour of individuals. Their activities on the internet and social media are also monitored. An individual's credit score is continuously updated based on their behaviour. Your credit score may determine your eligibility to avail of certain services. For instance, if your credit score falls below a certain level (say, 500), you may not be allowed to book train tickets. No, this is not a fiction. China has already started punishing people with low credit scores. The National Public Credit Information Centre of China reported that authorities banned people from purchasing air tickets 17.5 million times by the end of 2018.[2] Another tactic is naming and shaming. City authorities publish a blacklist of people with low scores and encourage companies to refer to the list before hiring or giving them contracts.

The AI-supported SCS is just one part of China's surveillance state. China is extensively collecting data on its citizens through online media and a network of more than 170 million CCTV cameras equipped with facial recognition capabilities.

Prima facie, the system looks innocuous with a noble aim of encouraging desirable behaviour by the citizens. However, in an authoritarian state, the definition of desirable behaviour may be vague and subjective. A protest against the government's discriminatory policies would be considered bad behaviour. Effectively, the basic right of citizens to voice their concerns is being taken away. Everyone is expected to be compliant with government rules and regulations, however unjust they may be.

China's AI Chatbot Trained on President Xi Jinping's Political Ideology

China has developed an AI chatbot trained on Xi Jinping Thought, reflecting the ideological constraints imposed on Chinese AI models.[3] In May 2024, China's cyberspace academy informed that the chatbot is trained on seven databases, with the seventh dedicated to Xi Jinping's doctrine of promoting socialism with Chinese characteristics. This initiative aligns with broader efforts to disseminate Xi's ideology, which includes mandatory classes in schools and the 'Study Xi, Strong Nation' app launched in 2019.

Xi Jinping Thought or Xi Jinping Thought on Socialism with Chinese Characteristics for a New Era encompasses 14 principles focused on the absolute power of the Chinese Communist Party, national security, socialist values and improving people's livelihoods. The AI model launched by the China Cyberspace Research Institute for internal use aims to demonstrate advancements in cybersecurity and IT research.

The chatbot can generate reports, summarize information and provide translations in Chinese and English. Users can select from among various knowledge bases for intelligent Q&A sessions, ensuring the content's professionalism and authority. This development underscores the integration of ideological education with AI technology, emphasizing the controlled and purposeful application of AI in China.

Obviously, China's AI chatbot, trained on Xi Jinping Thought, does not seem to be a responsible use of AI due to its ideological bias, promotion of propaganda, lack of transparency, suppression of intellectual freedom, and potential for misuse in surveillance and manipulation, thereby prioritizing political control over ethical AI principles.

AI is becoming very powerful thanks to the volumes of data being generated, collected and used to train AI models. With great power come great risks. This extremely potent tool can be used for good and bad. Unless used responsibly, AI can become a weapon against humanity. Considering the repercussions of misusing AI, a new area of study has emerged called responsible AI.

Responsible AI

Accenture defines responsible AI as 'the practice of designing, developing, and deploying AI with good intention to empower employees and businesses, and fairly impact customers and society—allowing companies to engender trust and scale AI with confidence.'[4] Using a responsible AI framework helps build the trust of employees and customers, infuse greater transparency, minimize biases in the AI model and protect data privacy and security.

The core elements of responsible AI, according to Accenture, revolve around the intention behind the design, development and deployment of AI systems. By emphasizing good intentions, companies are encouraged to prioritize positive outcomes and avoid unintended consequences. This commitment to ethical considerations is fundamental in establishing a foundation of trust internally and externally.

Transparency is a key pillar in responsible AI. It involves openly communicating how AI algorithms work, the data they use and the potential implications of their decisions. Providing this information fosters understanding among stakeholders, reduces uncertainty and allows for informed discussions regarding the ethical implications of AI applications.

Minimizing biases is another critical aspect of responsible AI. Biases within AI models can lead to unfair or discriminatory outcomes. Companies adopting a responsible AI framework actively work to identify and address biases in their algorithms, ensuring that AI applications treat individuals fairly and impartially.

Protecting data privacy and security is an integral part of responsible AI. Companies must establish robust measures to safeguard sensitive information, respecting individuals' privacy rights and meeting regulatory requirements. This not only upholds ethical standards but also mitigates the potential risks associated with unauthorized access to or misuse of data.

Developing Responsible AI

Leaders driving the use of AI in their organization need to understand the importance of responsible AI and follow a structured process for it. The Boston Consulting Group has identified the following six steps to develop responsible AI[5]:

1) Empower responsible AI leadership

    A chief AI ethics (CAIE) officer may be appointed to ensure the development of responsible AI. The CAIE officer may hold stakeholder consultations and establish principles and policies that guide the creation of AI systems. The officer may be assisted by a multidisciplinary team from different departments undertaking AI initiatives. The team may resolve complex ethical issues, such as bias and unintended consequences.

2) Develop principles, policies and training

    Organizations need to frame responsible AI principles in line with their vision, mission and corporate culture. It is a good practice to take a consultative approach in developing these principles by involving employees and addressing their concerns because AI may be seen as interfering with their privacy. These principles may be openly shared with employees to build their trust. People from the top level to end users need to be trained in responsible AI principles. Leaders need to encourage a culture of open communication where everyone is free to share their concerns, observations, findings and suggestions.

3) Establish human + AI governance

   Having drawn responsible AI principles, it is important to define roles, responsibilities and procedures to ensure that organizations incorporate responsible AI into their products and services. Responsible AI governance may include clear escalation paths for addressing project risks, standardized code reviews, designated individuals for handling concerns, and continuous improvements to rules and procedures to enhance capabilities and tackle new challenges during project delivery.

4) Conduct responsible AI reviews

   The outcome of the AI tool needs to be periodically reviewed to identify gaps, biases, risks and vulnerabilities. The review should be holistic in terms of data collection, model training, recommendations of the system and the action taken by the user. For example, if the AI recruitment tool recommends females more than males for a particular assignment, the tool's recommendations need to be reviewed for biases.

5) Integrate tools and methods

   The technical resources developing the AI system must be equipped with the tools and methods required to identify risks and vulnerabilities, such as biases of the model and possible misuse of the recommendations of the AI system. They should be trained in advanced tools available in the market for this purpose. Toolkits may consist of guidelines, procedures, tutorials, videos, checklists and standard stepwise processes to address common issues such as data bias and biased outcomes. These tools ensure that AI principles and policies are complied with and avoid resistance from the team in a timely manner. Indeed, without these tools, technical teams may find responsible AI principles an additional burden and may like to follow shortcuts.

6) Build and test a response plan

Although every step must be taken to avoid any lapse, leaders should be prepared for mistakes during the operation of an AI system. A response plan must be prepared to minimize the adverse impact of any unacceptable outcome of the AI system that might affect customers, employees or any other stakeholder. The plan should include steps to be taken to prevent further damage and rectify the issue, and a strategy to communicate with the stakeholders. A detailed plan with the roles and responsibilities of individuals for each stage helps in avoiding confusion instead of shifting responsibilities.

Challenges and Opportunities for Leaders of the VUCA World

How to ensure that the AI tool being used by my organization is following ethical and moral principles?

Adopting responsible AI poses challenges for business

leaders due to the complexity of aligning technological advancements with ethical considerations. Balancing innovation with accountability requires a nuanced understanding of AI systems, potential biases and privacy concerns. Executives must navigate evolving regulatory landscapes, invest in ethical training and establish transparent practices. Achieving this delicate balance demands a cultural shift within organizations, thereby emphasizing ethical values throughout the AI life cycle. Despite challenges, the adoption of responsible AI is imperative for building trust, avoiding reputational risks and ensuring long-term sustainable success in the rapidly evolving landscape of AI.

The unprecedented opportunities brought by AI cannot be tapped without ensuring the adoption of responsible AI. Businesses choosing responsible AI and going through the rigour of ensuring the ethical use of AI are likely to be more acceptable among customers and other stakeholders. Responsible AI may become a distinguishing feature of the service/product offered by a business to woo customers. For example, in 2021, Apple introduced a new privacy feature in iPhones—App Tracking Transparency (ATT)—which makes it harder for app-makers and advertisers to track user behaviour. In the absence of the iPhone user's consent, social media companies like Facebook (Meta) and X (formerly Twitter) cannot track the user and target them with personalized ads. ATT relies on responsible AI and asks for customers' consent before tracking their behaviour. This feature has become one of the most valuable USPs of iPhones over Android phones.

Embracing responsible AI not only aligns businesses

with ethical standards but also presents them with unique opportunities to gain a competitive edge. Customers, increasingly conscious of data privacy and ethical considerations, are inclined to favour companies that prioritize responsible AI practices. It becomes a distinguishing feature that enhances brand reputation and customer trust. For instance, Apple's introduction of the ATT feature showcases how responsibly leveraging AI for privacy concerns can become a valuable USP. Companies that proactively adopt responsible AI not only meet regulatory requirements but also differentiate themselves in the market, thus attracting a customer base that values transparency, the ethical use of technology and data protection. This shift towards responsible AI can position businesses as leaders in the evolving landscape, driving customer loyalty and market success.

'The ethical integration of artificial intelligence with human values and emotions is the foundation of future artificial intelligence.'

—Amit Ray

21

Data Quality and Governance

*'Data quality is directly linked to the
quality of decision-making.'*

—Melody Chien

SHARON CHRISTA MCAULIFFE WAS SELECTED FROM AMONG 11,000 teachers to be a part of the Challenger mission of the NASA programme called the Teacher in Space Project.[1] The then US president, Ronald Reagan, announced the programme in 1984 to inspire students, honour teachers and promote interest in mathematics, science and space exploration. She had planned to deliver two lessons through video from space to be broadcast on TV. McAuliffe was the first private citizen passenger in the history of space flight. She had undergone rigorous astronaut training for 120 days at the Johnson Space Center in Houston, Texas. The space shuttle was scheduled to be launched on 22 January 1986, but due to weather problems and technical issues, the launch was rescheduled for 28 January, 1986. Moments after take-off, the shuttle exploded, breaking into pieces in mid-air and throwing its occupants hurtling into the ocean from a height of 46,000 feet. All crew members, including McAuliffe, lost their lives. The Challenger disaster of 1986 was the darkest moment in the history of NASA's space missions.

President Reagan appointed an independent commission under the chairmanship of William P. Rogers to investigate the causes of the accident and make recommendations for corrective actions. The commission submitted its detailed report on 6 June 1986.[2] The report held NASA, its Marshall Space Flight Center in Huntsville, Alabama, and the contractor, Morton Thiokol Inc. in Ogden, Utah, responsible for the accident. The commission found that the failure was linked to an O-ring, a rubber seal, on the solid rocket boosters. The O-rings had degraded in the extremely cold weather of the launch, which caused superheated gases to vent through the seal. As a result, flammable gases escaped their containers and ignited, causing a disaster. The commission indicated that NASA managers were aware of the faulty design of the O-rings since 1977, but they did nothing about it. As per the report, the complete data on the impact of temperature on the O-rings were not considered in the analysis by NASA engineers. Data from only eight flights that had faced the erosion of O-rings were used to analyse the impact of low temperature on O-rings, as shown in Figure 21.1. The numbers (51-C, 41B, 61C, etc.) shown in the figure are the flight numbers.

From the below plot based on incomplete data (data only for flights that faced incidents of O-ring erosion), NASA engineers believed that there was no evidence of the impact of temperature on O-ring failures because incidences were spread across a large temperature range (50°F–75°F)

The report presented another plot using complete data from all flights, including those that had not faced an O-ring issue, as shown in Figure 21.2.

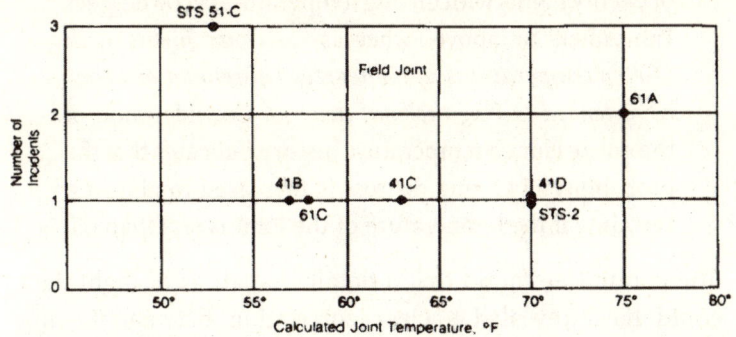

Figure 21.1[3]: Plot of flights with incidents of O-ring thermal distress as a function of temperature

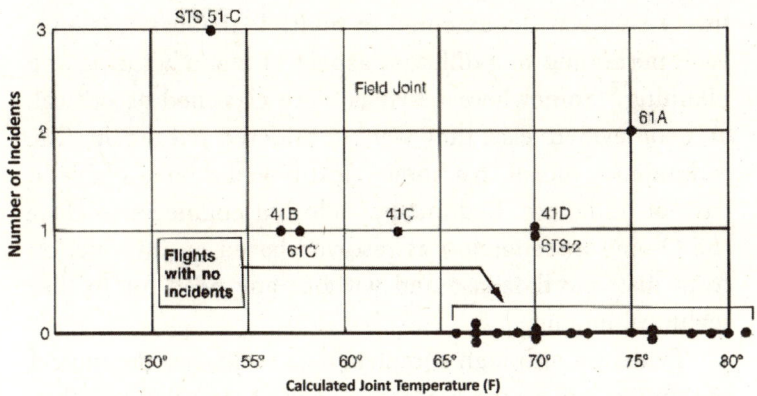

Figure 21.2[4]: Plot of flights with and without incidents of O-ring thermal distress as a function of temperature

Analysing the above plot, the committee mentioned[5]:

This comparison of flight history indicates that only three incidents of O-ring thermal distress occurred out of twenty flights with O-ring temperatures at 66 degrees Fahrenheit or above, whereas, *all four flights with O-ring temperatures at 63 degrees Fahrenheit or below experienced O-ring thermal distress.* Consideration of the entire launch temperature history indicates that the probability of O-ring distress is increased to almost a certainty if the temperature of the joint is less than 65.

The committee found that a detailed analysis of flight data could have revealed a clear correlation between O-ring damage and low temperatures. This failure to recognize the accurate relationship contributed to the faulty decision-making that ultimately led to the Challenger disaster. Another contributing factor was that the information about the O-ring was documented in multiple database systems, each pertaining to a different aspect of manufacturing and planning.[6] Somewhere, O-rings were classified as critical, and somewhere else, they were considered redundant. The redundancy meant that some backup would be available in case of its failure. Redundancy allowed engineers to close the O-ring investigation as resolved based on information from just one database and without any need for further technical enquiry.

Evidently, although complete data to analyse the impact of temperature on the performance of O-rings existed, they were fragmented across different databases. Consequently, incomplete data were used in the regression analysis done by NASA and the contractor (Morton Thiokol), which obviously provided flawed findings.

Other factors also contributed to the accident, as presented in the report. Nevertheless, this case is a classic example of how incomplete data and inconsistency in databases may result in a major disaster, causing the loss of precious human lives and loss of face for the US government and the world's number one space agency. For the families of the deceased astronauts and the students of McAuliffe, the incident would remain an unforgettable black spot in their memories. Data quality is of utmost importance to ensure desired outcomes.

The Loss of the Mars Climate Orbiter

On 11 December 1998, NASA launched the Mars Climate Orbiter (MCO) using a Delta II rocket from Launch Complex 17A at the Cape Canaveral Air Station in Florida to study the Martian climate, Martian atmosphere and surface changes on the planet. The spacecraft would take nine months to reach its intended orbit around Mars. On 23 September 1999, when the NASA team was planning to celebrate the success of the mission, luck was not in their favour. The spacecraft was lost while entering the Martian atmosphere on a lower-than-expected trajectory.

The MCO Mishap Investigation Board (MIB) conducted a root cause analysis of the accident. During a long journey, space scientists have to continuously monitor and adjust the spacecraft's trajectory to ensure that it stays on the intended path. The process of adjusting the trajectory by NASA involved transferring spacecraft data to the control centre on earth and then processing the data using the ground software SM_FORCE (Small Forces). The output file from SM_FORCE, called Angular Momentum Desaturation (AMD), was then used by the operations navigation team to estimate the forces acting on the spacecraft and adjust its trajectory by firing its thrusters as needed.

The MIB determined that the loss of the MCO was caused by an error in SM_FORCE's coding.[7] Specifically, the problem arose from using British units (pound-seconds) instead of metric units (kilogram-seconds) for the thruster performance data in the SM_FORCE software application code. The existing software interface documentation, which described data transfer between SM_FORCE and trajectory modeller software, required the data in the AMD file to be in metric units. As such, the trajectory modellers mistakenly assumed that the data provided were already in metric units as required. However, the output in the AMD file was in pound-seconds, which the machine on the spacecraft interpreted as Newton-seconds. This discrepancy led to the forces reported by the spacecraft engineers for orbit determination solutions being underestimated by a factor of 4.45 (1 pound force equals 4.45 Newtons). This meant that the AMD software underestimated the effects of the spacecraft thrusters by a factor of 4.45 in every impulse measurement. This error accumulated with every trajectory correction over nine months. Finally, on the day of the planned Mars insertion, the actual spacecraft trajectory was just 56 km from the surface of Mars instead of the estimated trajectory of 226 km, as shown in Figure 21.3; the MCO burned into the Martian atmosphere. The minimum safe distance from Mars' surface for the spacecraft was 80 km.

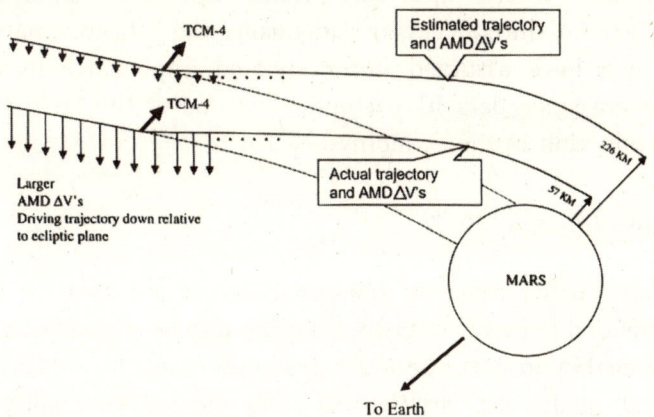

Figure 21.3[8]: Schematic MCO encounter diagram (not to scale)

The case reflects how an inconsistency in the units of data used by the two systems resulted in a disaster involving millions of dollars ($125 million in this case). This was a major data quality issue wherein different databases were interpreting the same data in different units. It is similar to if a product priced in dollars has a price tag in rupees without converting dollars to rupees. So, a 100-dollar product would be shown as a 100-rupee product on the e-commerce website, thus undermining the actual cost by 1/80th (considering $1 = INR 80). Obviously, this kind of inadequacy in data quality may be devastating for any business.

From the above two examples, it is evident that the consistency of data being used for any application is very crucial for fruitful and trustworthy outcomes.[9] Garbage in, garbage out is always true in the context of data, which means nonsense input data produce nonsense output. Let us explore the concepts of data quality and data governance, which have assumed unprecedented importance in the AI era since data have emerged as one of the factors of production in the economy.

Data Quality

Data quality refers to the suitability of the data for the intended purpose. Data are considered to be of good quality when they are accurate and truly represent real-life scenarios. High-quality data are the real gold, whereas low-quality or inaccurate data are like debris, which may not only present an incorrect picture but also be disastrous, as we have seen in the case of the NASA Challenger Mission in 1986 and Mars Climate Orbiter in 1999. The main characteristics of good-quality data are as follows:

Accuracy: The data should be correct and should pertain to real-world situations. A reliable source of data is essential to ensure data accuracy.

Completeness: The dataset should be comprehensive to represent all scenarios for which the data have been captured. An analysis based on incomplete data may not be reliable and workable as seen in the NASA Challenger Mission failure—the impact of temperature on O-rings was analysed using incomplete data, excluding flights without O-ring failures.

Consistency: In the context of data quality, consistency means that a piece of information doesn't contradict another piece of information in a different database, source or system. For example, an individual's name should be the same in all the databases of an organization. As seen earlier, a data reliability issue led to the failure of the NASA Challenger Mission in 1986 wherein O-rings were classified differently in different databases.

Relevance: This refers to the usefulness of data. Is the information really needed for the intended purpose? Collecting or processing data that are not needed would only waste energy and result in low-quality data.

Validity: Data should be collected according to the business rules and parameters defined by the organization.

Uniqueness: This ensures there is no duplication or overlapping of values across all datasets.

Timeliness: This refers to whether the data are up to date and present the most recent situation. If there is some change in the situation for which data have not been updated, the data would not serve the desired purpose. The data should be available when needed. For some applications, data may be needed on a real-time basis.

Needless to mention, data quality is of utmost importance for data-driven decision-making for an organization in the AI era. Maintaining and ensuring data quality is not an easy task. Although numerous digital tools are available for cleaning, monitoring and managing data quality, a data governance (DG) framework may be quite effective in ensuring the quality.

Data Governance

Data governance refers to the establishment of rules, standards and policies to define how data are sourced, collected, cleaned, processed and disposed of after they complete their life cycle. It includes ways to ensure that the data are secure, consistent, private, accurate, available and usable, that is, data quality is good. It also includes the processes to be followed and technologies to be used by people to ensure good data quality throughout the data life cycle.

Leaders of the VUCA world need to have a DG framework to manage data on an ongoing basis, through which a single set of rules and processes can be developed for collecting, storing and using data, thus ensuring data quality.

Challenges and Opportunities for Leaders of the VUCA World

How to ensure the availability of good quality data?

The difference between useful data and useless data is the same as between gold and sand. Although a very small quantity of gold may be found in sand, sand cannot fulfil the utility of gold. Likewise, poor-quality data can not only be useless but also decisions taken based on such data may be disastrous for the organization.

The challenge before the leaders of the VUCA world is to extract good-quality data that are accurate, complete, consistent, relevant, valid, unique and timely available. They can provide invaluable insights into the business, enabling data-driven decisions that can drive performance, reduce costs, minimize mistakes and ultimately improve customer satisfaction.

Creating a DG framework is an instrumental step in

ensuring data quality. This framework establishes rules, policies and procedures for data management, ensuring that data are properly collected, analysed, stored and shared. By adopting a DG framework, businesses can ensure that the data they rely on are trustworthy and of the highest quality, enabling them to make informed decisions and stay competitive in the AI era.

Having high-quality data are essential for making sound business decisions and present a significant opportunity for businesses to improve performance and gain a competitive edge. By having quality data, businesses can optimize costs, reduce errors, create better products and services and better understand their customers' needs and preferences. Moreover, companies that lack quality data risk losing out on valuable insights that could help them stay ahead of the competition.

The importance of data quality cannot be overstated in today's VUCA business environment. Businesses that invest in data quality will be better equipped to survive and thrive in the AI era, whereas those that neglect it may struggle to keep up.

Conclusively, data quality is the key to unlock the full potential of data in the AI era. Just as gold is more valuable than sand, good-quality data are the foundation of effective decision-making and business performance. By investing in a DG framework and prioritizing data quality, leaders can gain a competitive advantage and position their businesses for long-term success.

'Good quality data provides better leads, better understanding of customers and better customer relationships. Data quality is a competitive advantage that D&A [data and analytics] leaders need to improve upon continuously.'

—Melody Chien

22

The Blue Screen Catastrophe

'No longer are technology and cyber issues confined to tech geeks in some backroom. In the digital age, IT issues are front and centre. They are central to what government does and how it does it.'

—Will Hurd

IN AN ERA WHERE DIGITAL TECHNOLOGY DRIVES INNOVATION and efficiency, dependency on interconnected systems has never been greater. The global outage of the Microsoft Windows operating system in July 2024 due to a flawed update from cybersecurity firm CrowdStrike is a stark reminder of the challenges inherent in large-scale digitalization and the dangers of placing too much trust in a single system. This incident not only disrupted industries worldwide but also highlighted the vulnerabilities that come with our heavy reliance on digital platforms. This chapter discusses the event, its impact and the lessons learned for mitigating such risks in the future from the perspective of challenges and opportunities for new-age leadership.

CrowdStrike and Its Association with Microsoft

CrowdStrike is a cybersecurity company specializing in protecting organizations from various digital threats. They use a powerful software platform called Falcon to monitor and secure computer systems. CrowdStrike provides important security services to Microsoft. It helps watch over Microsoft 365 and Azure (Microsoft's cloud services) to detect any suspicious activities and stop potential cyberattacks. This includes checking log files (records of activities) to ensure they are accurate, which is crucial for investigations and legal matters.

The Incident

On 19 July 2024, at 04.09 GMT, a routine update from CrowdStrike, intended to enhance threat detection capabilities, inadvertently triggered a catastrophic global outage of the Microsoft Windows operating system. The update, designed to bolster the Falcon sensor's ability to gather telemetry on new cyberthreats, caused a massive wave of Windows system crashes, commonly known as the Blue Screen of Death.

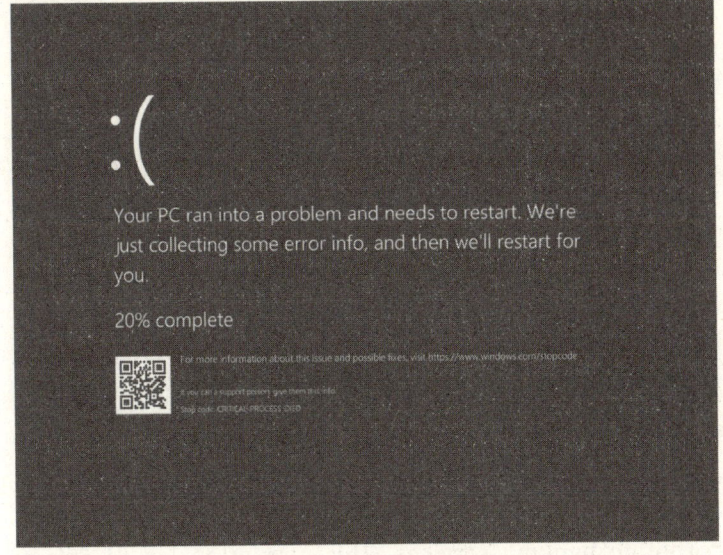

The blue screen of death[1]

Within an hour, from 04.09 to 05.27 GMT, systems across the globe experienced severe disruptions. While Mac and Linux systems were unaffected, Windows hosts that were online during this period were hit hard, causing widespread chaos.

The Ripple Effect

This outage had an unprecedentedly far-reaching impact. According to reports, the affected sectors faced severe financial losses.[2] This incident had profound effects on critical sectors like healthcare, banking, aviation and government services.

Healthcare sector: The healthcare industry faced severe disruptions because hospitals and medical facilities struggled to access electronic health records and other critical systems. This led to delays in patient care, diagnostic procedures and treatment plans. The inability to access vital patient information in real time posed serious risks, particularly for patients requiring urgent care. Financially, the healthcare sector bore significant losses of around $1.94 billion. The downtime affected not only routine operations but also emergency services, compounding the challenges faced by healthcare providers.

Banking sector: The banking industry also suffered considerable setbacks due to the outage. Banks experienced difficulties in processing transactions, affecting retail and corporate banking services. This disruption led to delays in financial transactions, impacting customers' ability to access funds and conduct business. Additionally, ATMs and online banking services were intermittently unavailable, causing frustration among customers. The financial impact on the banking sector was estimated at approximately $1.15 billion. The outage highlighted the vulnerability of financial institutions to IT disruptions and the need for robust contingency plans.

Aviation sector: Airlines were among the hardest hit by the glitch. Major carriers had to cancel or delay numerous flights, leading to travel chaos for thousands of passengers. Airport operations were disrupted because check-in systems, boarding processes and baggage handling were affected by the outage. Major airlines, including American Airlines and United Airlines, and several Indian carriers, such as SpiceJet,

Air India and IndiGo, experienced operational difficulties, compounding the crisis. The aviation sector faced substantial financial losses due to operational disruptions and costs associated with compensating affected passengers. The outage highlighted the critical dependence of the aviation industry on reliable IT systems for smooth operations.

Government services: The outage also impacted government services, including emergency response systems. Government agencies faced challenges in accessing essential data and coordinating response efforts. This disruption posed risks to public safety and highlighted the critical need for resilient IT infrastructure in government operations.

The total estimated financial impact of the outage was around $5 billion, reflecting the extensive downtime and operational challenges across multiple sectors. The incident highlighted the interconnectedness of modern IT systems and cascading effects that a single point of failure can have on various industries.

Measures Taken by CrowdStrike

As per the CrowdStrike Preliminary Post Incident Review posted by CrowdStrike on its website, it has taken a slew of measures to prevent the recurrence of such events in the future, as shown in the box below.[3]

> **Box 22.0: CrowdStrike strategy to prevent recurrence of such an event**
>
> - **Enhanced Software Testing Procedures**
>   - » Improve Rapid Response Content testing by using testing types such as local developer, content update and rollback, stress, fuzzing, fault injection, stability, and content interface testing.
>   - » Introduce additional validation checks in the Content Validator to prevent similar issues.
>
> - **Enhanced Resilience and Recoverability**
>   - » Strengthen error handling mechanisms in the Falcon sensor to ensure errors from problematic content are managed gracefully.
>
> - **Refined Deployment Strategy**
>   - » Adopt a staggered deployment strategy, starting with a canary deployment to a small subset of systems before a further staged rollout.
>   - » Enhance monitoring of sensor and system performance during the staggered content deployment to identify and mitigate issues promptly.
>   - » Provide customers with greater control over the delivery of Rapid Response Content updates by allowing granular selection of when and where these updates are deployed.
>   - » Provide notifications of content updates and timing.
>
> - **Third Party Validation**
>   - » Conduct multiple independent third-party security code reviews.
>   - » Conduct independent reviews of end-to-end quality processes from development through deployment.

Microsoft's Central Role

At the heart of the disruption was Microsoft's Windows operating system, which serves as the backbone for countless enterprises and individuals worldwide. The outage highlighted the risks associated with centralizing critical functions within a single platform. Microsoft's dominance in the operating system market means that any significant flaw or issue in its environment can have cascading effects across multiple sectors.

When such a system falters, the ripple effects can be felt globally, affecting millions of users and businesses.

The CrowdStrike–Microsoft outage serves as a powerful reminder of the vulnerabilities inherent in our increasingly digital world. As technology continues to evolve and integrate more deeply into every facet of our lives, the risks associated with digitalization must be carefully managed. By implementing robust testing and validation processes, diversifying technology dependencies, and enhancing monitoring and response strategies, organizations can better navigate the challenges of digitalization and safeguard against potential disruptions. The lessons learned from this incident will be crucial in shaping a resilient and secure digital future.

Role of Leaders in Navigating the Risks of Digitalization

The CrowdStrike–Microsoft outage serves as a critical lesson for business leaders about the complexities and risks of digitalization. As organizations continue to integrate advanced technologies and rely on interconnected systems, leaders must be vigilant and proactive in managing digital risks.

Ultimately, the role of business leaders extends beyond managing day-to-day operations. It encompasses strategic oversight, technological stewardship and proactive leadership to safeguard against potential disruptions and ensure organizational resilience. Here's how business leaders can play a pivotal role in mitigating risks and ensuring resilience in the AI era.

Strategic Oversight and Risk Management

- **Embrace a risk-aware culture:** Business leaders must cultivate a culture that prioritizes risk awareness and management. This involves fostering an environment wherein potential risks are openly discussed and addressed. By promoting a culture that values proactive risk management, leaders can help ensure that vulnerabilities are identified and mitigated before they lead to significant disruptions.
- **Develop comprehensive risk management strategies:** Leaders should oversee the development of robust risk management strategies that address technological and operational risks. This includes evaluating the potential impact of system failures and implementing measures to reduce dependency on any single platform or provider. Regular risk assessments and scenario planning can help anticipate and prepare for potential disruptions.
- **Invest in resilience and redundancy:** Strategic investments in resilience and redundancy are crucial for mitigating the impact of digital

disruptions. Business leaders should ensure that their organizations have contingency plans, backup systems and alternative solutions to maintain operations during unforeseen outages. Investing in redundant systems and diverse technology providers can also help reduce the risks associated with dependency on a single platform.

Technological Stewardship

- **Prioritize robust testing and validation:** Business leaders must advocate for and support rigorous testing and validation processes. This includes ensuring that updates and new technologies undergo thorough testing to identify and address potential issues before deployment. Leaders should work closely with the IT and cybersecurity teams to implement comprehensive testing protocols and validation checks.
- **Foster innovation with caution:** Although embracing innovation is essential to stay competitive, business leaders should balance innovation with caution. Rapid technological advancements should be managed carefully to avoid introducing vulnerabilities. Leaders should encourage innovation within a framework that emphasizes security, stability and thorough vetting.
- **Enhance monitoring and incident response:** Effective monitoring and incident response capabilities are critical for managing digital risks. Business leaders should invest in advanced monitoring tools and systems that provide real-

time insights into system performance and potential threats. Additionally, leaders should ensure that incident response plans are well defined and regularly practised to minimize the impact of disruptions.

Proactive Leadership and Communication

- **Lead by example:** Business leaders set the tone for their organizations. By prioritizing security and risk management at the highest levels, they can influence organizational behaviour and decision-making. Leading by example involves making informed decisions about technology investments, advocating for best practices and demonstrating a commitment to safeguarding the organization's digital assets.
- **Engage with stakeholders:** Open and transparent communication with stakeholders, including customers, partners and employees, is essential during and after a digital disruption. Business leaders should ensure that stakeholders are informed about the potential risks, disruptions and recovery plans. Clear communication helps build trust and demonstrates a commitment to addressing challenges effectively.
- **Champion continuous improvement:** The digital landscape is constantly evolving and so are the associated risks. Business leaders should champion a culture of continuous improvement by regularly reviewing and updating risk management strategies, testing procedures and incident response plans. Emphasizing the importance of learning from past incidents and implementing improvements

ensures that the organization remains resilient and adaptable.

Challenges and Opportunities for Leaders of the VUCA World

How to protect my organization from global events?

The AI era has revolutionized business operations, offering unprecedented efficiency and innovation while also presenting significant risks. The Microsoft global outage caused by a flawed update from CrowdStrike highlights the challenges and opportunities inherent in our increasingly digital world.

The incident depicted how a single software update can lead to widespread disruptions across various sectors, underscoring the vulnerabilities inherent in modern systems. Another major challenge is the rapid pace of technological advancement, which often outstrips our ability to thoroughly test and validate new technologies. This gap can create security vulnerabilities that are exploited by cyberthreats. Further, heavily relying on a single platform, such as Microsoft Windows, increases the risk of widespread disruptions if that platform experiences issues or vulnerabilities. As digital threats become more frequent and sophisticated, there is growing pressure to maintain robust security measures and comply with increasingly strict regulations. This complex interplay of factors highlights the importance of continually evolving security measures to address the technological and regulatory challenges of the AI era.

Leaders can turn challenges into opportunities and develop a competitive advantage by adopting robust risk mitigation measures. Investing in advanced system management and monitoring tools improves operational reliability and efficiency, offering a stable service that distinguishes the organization from its competitors. Adopting agile risk management frameworks enables swift adaptation to technological changes and emerging threats, positioning the organization as a leader in innovation and responsiveness. Diversifying technology infrastructure reduces dependency on single platforms, increasing resilience and operational stability, which can be promoted as a competitive strength. Resilient innovation in tandem with risk management fosters a culture that supports creativity and stability, setting the organization apart in market trends. Finally, robust incident response capabilities ensure minimal downtime and recovery time during crises, thereby building customer confidence and operational continuity. By focusing on these areas, organizations can transform digital challenges into strategic advantages to enhance their market position and achieve long-term success.

> 'The digital world has power because it has dynamic information, but it's important that we stay human instead of being another machine sitting in front of a machine.'
>
> —Pranav Mistry

23

Digital Transformation

'In the digital age, digital transformation must be at the heart of every enterprise, whereby they leverage digital technologies to improve efficiency, enhance customer experience and produce value to its markets.'

—Sally Njeri Wangari

Amazon's Digital Transformation

Amazon started as an online marketplace for books in 1994 with a mission to offer customers a vast selection at competitive prices and to make shopping for books as convenient as possible. Over time, Amazon underwent a remarkable digital transformation, propelling it to become one of the world's largest and most prosperous e-commerce platforms.

Initially, customers could only buy physical books from Amazon's website. However, as the company expanded, it started adding other products to its inventory, including electronics, clothing and home goods. It also created its own brands, which enabled it to offer a wide range of products at competitive prices. By the late 1990s, Amazon emerged as one of the largest and most popular online retailers.

Nevertheless, Amazon's quest for digital transformation didn't stop there. In 2007, the company unveiled Amazon Prime, a subscription service. It offered members unlimited one-day delivery on eligible items along with access to streaming services for music and movies. This service turned out to be incredibly popular and facilitated more sales for the company. Prime members were also offered other benefits such as early access to lightning deals, free e-books, and more.

Along with expanding its product offerings and introducing new services, Amazon focused on new technologies, including AI and ML. It used these technologies to enhance customer experience in numerous ways. For example, it developed advanced algorithms to make personalized product recommendations to shoppers based on their browsing and purchase history. It also introduced one of the most advanced AI virtual assistants, Alexa, which could help customers with their shopping needs.

In later years, Amazon entered new markets such as healthcare, advertising and grocery delivery. In 2017, it acquired Whole Foods, an organic grocery chain, which enabled it to expand its presence in the grocery market and offer a wide selection of fresh food and household essentials to its customers. The company also began offering advertising solutions to other businesses and brands that wanted to access Amazon's huge customer base.

Amazon Web Services (AWS), its cloud computing arm, was another area of digitalization. AWS helped the company further diversify its revenue stream. The platform offers a wide range of services, including storage, databases and analytics, to other companies and organizations, which allows them to quickly and easily scale their operations.

One of the most noteworthy examples of Amazon's digital transformation is its focus on automation and efficiency. Since its early days, the company has been investing in technologies to optimize its operations and improve its bottom line. For example, Amazon uses radio frequency identification (RFID) tags to track inventory and ensure that products are always in stock. It also uses sophisticated algorithms to optimize its logistics and supply chain processes, which enables it to make products available to customers as quickly and cheaply as possible. It acquired warehouse robotics company Kiva to optimize its warehousing systems.[1] In 2014, Amazon installed over 15,000 robots in its US warehouses to get ready to deal with peak demand during the holiday season.

Presently, Amazon's business has surpassed its original idea of online shopping. It has become a major player in a wide range of industries, including e-commerce, cloud computing, online advertising, digital streaming and AI. It continues to push the boundaries of what is possible in the AI era, and its ongoing digital transformation is a testament to its innovative spirit and commitment to customer satisfaction.

Amazon's story is an example of how digital transformation can help a company grow and thrive in today's fast-paced, highly connected digital world. By constantly innovating and embracing digital technologies, Amazon has digitally transformed itself from a simple online bookstore into one of the world's largest and most successful e-commerce platforms. The company's ability to adopt, adapt and evolve over the years is a testament to its leadership, vision and determination to succeed. The story of Amazon's digital transformation serves as an inspiration for other companies looking to digitally transform their businesses.

Digital Transformation of a Legacy Company: General Electric

Digital transformation is not the forte of only new-age companies. Even more century-old companies are redefining themselves as digital companies. General Electric (GE) is one of them. GE is a multinational conglomerate that has undergone a notable digital transformation in recent years. The company, founded in 1892, has a long history of innovation. It has been a leader in many industries, including energy, aviation and healthcare.

In the early 2010s, GE realized the potential of digital technologies and started investing heavily in them. One of the first steps it took was to create GE Digital in 2015. GE Digital focused on developing and commercializing software and analytics solutions. In the words of Jeffrey Immelt, chairman and CEO, GE, 'As GE transforms itself to become the world's premier digital industrial company, this will provide GE's customers with the best industrial solutions and the software needed to solve real-world problems. It will make GE a digital show site and grow our software and analytics enterprise from $6 billion in 2015 to a top 10 software company by 2020.'[2] GE Digital quickly grew and began generating significant revenue for the company.

GE also invested heavily in IoT, sensors and connected devices because it recognized the potential of these technologies to improve efficiency and optimize costs across its various industries. The company began embedding sensors and connectivity into its products, such as jet engines and wind turbines, which allowed real-time monitoring and data collection.

Another notable aspect of GE's digital transformation strategy was the adoption of a data-driven approach to decision-making. The company invested in analytics and ML capabilities, which enabled it to process and analyse the vast amounts of data generated by its connected devices. These data were very handy in optimizing operations, improving product design and identifying new revenue streams.

GE Digital is a leader in digital solutions across a range of industries. In electric utilities, its software optimizes grid management for reliability. The power generation sector benefits from enhanced efficiency and predictive maintenance. In oil and gas, GE Digital facilitates data-driven decision-making for exploration and refining processes. Its solutions have revolutionized manufacturing and digital plant operations by streamlining processes and reducing downtime. Furthermore, GE Digital has played a pivotal role in aviation by optimizing fleet management and operational efficiency for safer air travel. Across these sectors, GE Digital's commitment to innovation, efficiency and sustainability has positioned it as a front runner in digital transformation. Its comprehensive suite of solutions, which fosters operational excellence and embraces the power of digital technology for a diverse range of applications, caters to industry-specific needs.

GE's digital transformation has had a significant impact on the company's bottom line. GE Digital has emerged as a major contributor to the company's revenue and has helped drive growth across the business. IoT and data analytics capabilities have also led to significant cost savings and improved operational efficiency.

Overall, GE's digital transformation has been a success story, demonstrating the potential of digital technologies to drive growth and improve business operations.

Digital Transformation of Customer Experience: DMRC

The Delhi Metro Rail Corporation's (DMRC) vision is, 'Commuting experience in Delhi Metro to be customer's delight.' Embracing the era of technology, DMRC has implemented a plethora of digital initiatives aimed at streamlining various aspects of its services to enhance customer experience. A notable advancement is the digitalization of ticketing processes. Passengers now have access to multiple channels for purchasing tickets, including its own mobile app—Momentum 2.0 Delhi Sarthi, WhatsApp, PayTM, PhonePe, Amazon Pay and IRCTC Rail Connect app/website. This not only enhances convenience but also reduces the reliance on traditional ticketing methods. There are multiple fare medias, which include the National Common Mobility Card (NCMC), DMRC smart card, single-journey QR ticket and multiple-journey QR (MJQR) ticket.

Furthermore, digital payment options, such as UPI, credit/debit cards and net banking, have been seamlessly integrated into the ticketing system, offering passengers a hassle-free and secure way to pay for their journeys.

Moreover, the introduction of an AI-based chatbot CHETNA (Chatbot for Efficient Transit Navigation and Assistance) has transformed how passengers interact with DMRC. This virtual assistant provides instant responses to enquiries, offers real-time updates on metro services and provides personalized guidance to passengers, contributing to a smooth and efficient commuting experience.

DMRC employs predictive maintenance for critical assets, including tracks, rolling stock, signalling systems, lifts, escalators and traction systems. This proactive approach ensures improved reliability, reduced downtime and cost-effective management of its infrastructure and operational efficiency.

Overall, the digital transformation initiatives undertaken by DMRC have significantly improved passenger experience, making the Delhi Metro a shining example of technological innovation in public transportation.

Challenges and Opportunities for Leaders of the VUCA World

How to digitally transform my organization?

The above examples of contemporary and legacy companies demonstrate the need for digitalization for any business today. Leaders of the AI era will have to digitally transform their businesses to stay afloat in a tsunami of digital revolutions. Those who manage to leverage the huge opportunities provided by digitalization will emerge as market leaders. The most challenging question is to find ways to digitally transform their businesses.

How to digitally transform your business?

There are several key steps that leaders can take to digitally transform their organization:

- Develop a digital strategy: This involves identifying specific business areas for improvement through digital technologies and outlining actionable steps to achieve those improvements. It includes setting clear goals and defining KPIs to effectively monitor, measure and evaluate the progress and performance of the targeted areas over time.
- Invest in technology: Once you have a clear idea of what you want to achieve, you can start investing in the technology and tools that will help you get there. This could include cloud computing, automation tools and data analytics software.
- Embrace data: Data are one of the most powerful tools that businesses have for driving digital transformation. Invest in data management and analytics tools, and make sure that your team is trained to use them effectively.
- Empower your employees: Digital transformation requires a change in mindset and culture. Employees should be trained in new technologies and given the necessary tools to efficiently perform their job.
- Create a customer-centric culture: Put the customer at the centre of your business. Use technology such as data analytics, ML and AI to get a better understanding of your customers' needs and

preferences, and use that information to improve their experience.
- Continuously monitor and improve: Digital transformation is an ongoing process, so it is important to continuously monitor and measure the progress you are making and make adjustments as necessary.

Overall, the key to successful digital transformation is to have a clear vision of what you want to achieve, invest in the right technology and be willing to embrace change. The appropriate step in this process is to develop a digital transformation strategy.

Digital Transformation Strategy

A digital transformation strategy is a plan for an organization to use technology to fundamentally change how it operates and delivers value to its customers. This often involves adopting new technologies and digital tools, such as cloud computing, data analytics and automation, to improve efficiency, drive innovation and enhance customer engagement. A successful digital transformation strategy must be aligned with the organization's overall business goals and objectives and may involve changes to organizational structure, processes and culture.

Broadly speaking, the strategy may focus on four key areas: customer experience, operations, products and services, and internal business processes.

Customer Experience

Customer experience now revolves around leveraging digital tools like digital marketing, service delivery and customer relations management to delight consumers. Amazon's digital transformation is a prime illustration of customer-centric digitalization. Through innovative digital marketing strategies, seamless digital service delivery and efficient digital customer relations management, Amazon has redefined the online shopping experience. This approach not only enhances convenience but also personalizes interactions, contributing to customer satisfaction and loyalty. Amazon's success showcases the pivotal role of digital tools in shaping customer experience and illustrates how a customer-focused digital strategy can drive business excellence in the contemporary market. Similarly, DMRC enhanced customer experience by deploying a slew of digital initiatives.

Operations

The digitalization of operations involves transformative measures such as predictive demand forecasting, demand-driven operations, real-time monitoring and the predictive maintenance of assets. By implementing these strategies, businesses aim to enhance availability, reduce costs and redefine KPIs through digital monitoring systems. GE Digital, as discussed earlier, is particularly focused on advancing the digitalization of operations. This focus underscores its commitment to leveraging digital technologies for predictive analytics, real-time insights and optimized asset management, thereby aligning with the industry trend of efficient, data-driven and technologically advanced operational practices.

Delivery of Products and Services

Digitalizing product and service delivery involves leveraging IoT devices, connected products, pay-per-use models and shared services. IoT devices enable seamless connectivity, and connected products enhance user experience. Pay-per-use models offer flexible payment structures, and shared services facilitate collaborative consumption. Embracing these digital strategies transforms traditional delivery methods by optimizing efficiency and meeting evolving consumer preferences in the rapidly digitalizing market.

Internal Business Processes

The digitalization of business processes involves adopting transformative technologies, such as enterprise resource planning, enabling work from anywhere, establishing virtual workplaces, implementing digital HR management and integrating various systems digitally. These initiatives streamline operations, enhance collaboration and improve the overall efficiency of a company's internal processes. Embracing these digital tools modernizes organizational workflows and facilitates adaptability to evolving work paradigms, fostering an agile and responsive business environment.

A summary of sample strategies for each area is presented in Table 23.0.

Table 23.0: Digital transformation

Area	Digital Strategy
Digitalize Customer Experience	Digital Marketing Digital Experience Digital Services Post-sales Services
Digitalize Operations	Demand-driven Operations Value Chain Integration Real-time Monitoring Predictive Maintenance Redefine KPIs
Digitalize Delivery of Products and Services	Shared Services Pay-per-use Model Connected Products Sensors in Products
Digitalize Internal Business Processes	Enterprise Resource Planning Remote Work Virtual Workplaces Digital HR Management Digital Performance Monitoring Robust Data Security System

In today's rapidly evolving digital world, businesses are under increasing pressure to keep up with the digital revolution. A digital transformation is no longer an option but a necessity for businesses to survive and thrive in this ever-changing landscape.

Data security remains the common denominator among all these digital technologies.

Investing in technology and empowering employees with the necessary tools and training is crucial for a successful digital transformation. Data are one of the most valuable assets in the AI era, and businesses must embrace them to gain insights that can help them make data-driven decisions. Creating a customer-centric culture is also critical, as this can help businesses better understand their customers' needs and preferences and improve their overall experience.

Successful digital transformation is an ongoing process that requires continuous monitoring and improvement. The pace of change in the AI era is relentless, and businesses must be willing to adapt and evolve to remain relevant. With a clear vision, the right technology investments and a willingness to embrace change, businesses can successfully transform themselves and stay ahead of the competition.

'There is an alternative to digital transformation, digital extinction.'

—Dwayne Mulenga Isaac, Jr

Afterword

As we come to an end of this journey about the digital frontier, we reflect on the myriad challenges and boundless opportunities that define leadership in the AI era. Our exploration has traversed the landscapes of technology, strategy, culture and innovation, shedding light on the essential qualities and skills required of leaders in the ever-evolving digital landscape.

Amidst uncertainty and volatility, leaders are called upon to be agile, innovative and strategic. They must possess a deep understanding of technology and its potential to drive business objectives and the ability to navigate ambiguity with clarity and confidence. Data analytics skills, which enable leaders to unlock insights and drive organizational success, have emerged as indispensable tools for decision-making.

Throughout our journey, we have confronted the challenges inherent in the AI era head-on. From the complexities of data governance to the imperatives of aligning organizational structures and cultures with the new paradigm of automation, leaders are tasked with smartly navigating a landscape fraught with pitfalls and opportunities alike. The spectres of online fraud, biases in models and data security loom large, underscoring the critical importance of ethical considerations and the responsible use of technology.

Nevertheless, boundless opportunities for growth and innovation lie amidst these challenges. Digitalization offers the promise of improved efficiency, increased market share and competitive advantage. By embracing technology, leaders can delight customers, drive organizational success and emerge as market leaders in their respective domains.

Our journey has drawn parallels with historical challenges and the innovations that emerged from them. From the invention of electricity to the development of the first electronic computer, history teaches us that adversity breeds innovation. In the crucible of the Second World War, humanity witnessed the birth of transformative technologies such as the jet engine, radar and microwave oven. Similarly, the discovery of penicillin revolutionized medicine, saving countless lives from infections. As we stand on the precipice of the AI era, we are called upon to harness the transformative power of technology to confront the challenges of our time.

The future promises even greater possibilities. The advent of generative AI, such as ChatGPT, represents a quantum leap in human–machine interaction. These models hold the potential to augment human capabilities, thus enabling us to unlock new frontiers of knowledge and creativity. By embracing cutting-edge technologies, leaders can leverage these advancements to drive innovation and shape the future of their organizations.

In conclusion, the AI era presents significant challenges and opportunities. By investing in advanced system management, agile risk frameworks, diverse infrastructures and robust security measures, business leaders can smartly navigate complexities, enhance resilience and gain a competitive edge, hence ensuring long-term success in an increasingly digital landscape.

We are also reminded that leadership in the AI era is not merely about navigating technological complexities but also about inspiring and empowering teams to achieve their full potential. It is about fostering a culture of continuous learning, adaptability and strategic thinking. It is also about embracing change with courage and conviction, knowing that the only constant in the AI era is change itself which is happening at record-breaking speed.

We thank our readers for accompanying us on this journey. We hope our book has served as a guiding light, illuminating the path towards leadership excellence in the digital landscape. May you continue embracing the challenges and opportunities of the digital frontier with optimism, resilience and resolve. In the crucible of the AI era, smart leaders will be forged and new horizons await those bold enough to seize them.

As we bid farewell to this book, we eagerly anticipate the next, knowing that the journey towards leadership excellence is an ongoing odyssey fuelled by curiosity, courage and the relentless pursuit of innovation.

Farewell, fellow travellers, and may your quest for leadership excellence in the AI era be met with success and fulfilment.

Acknowledgements

We extend our heartfelt gratitude to those who have supported, motivated, inspired and guided us throughout the journey of writing this book.

To our friends, family members and colleagues, your relentless support and encouragement have been a constant source of motivation. Your belief in us and your words of encouragement have propelled us forward during moments of doubt.

We are immensely grateful for the vast amount of information available online that has been instrumental in shaping our understanding and perspectives. This wealth of knowledge has enriched our research and broadened our horizons.

To all those who have shared their insights, provided feedback and contributed to our understanding of the topics discussed in this book, we express our deepest appreciation. Your guidance has been invaluable in shaping the content and ensuring its relevance and accuracy.

Thank you to each and every individual who has played a part, big or small, in the creation of this book. Your support has been integral to its completion, and we are profoundly grateful for your contribution to this endeavour.

Thank you.

References

INTRODUCTION

1. Zaidi, Tarab, 'US Flight Glitch: Unspecified Personnel Corrupted Data File Leading to FAA Outage, Says Report', *Business Today*, 13 January 2023, https://tinyurl.com/4w8vr6er. Accessed on 14 January 2023.
2. Sharma, Devyanshi, 'Lawyer Faces Trouble After Using ChatGPT for Research, AI Tool Comes Up with Fake Cases That Never Existed', *India Today*, 28 May 2023, https://tinyurl.com/ywvuj7kx. Accessed on 12 May 2024.

CHAPTER 1: DATA: A NEW FACTOR OF PRODUCTION

1. Nassiri, Alessandro, 'Enigma', *Wikimedia Commons*, 20 April 2016, https://tinyurl.com/3ukpsfhw. Accessed on 18 June 2024.
2. Copeland, B.J., 'Alan Turing: British Mathematician and Logician', *Britannica*, 19 June 2024, https://tinyurl.com/4fucdtez. Accessed on 18 June 2024.
3. Goodwin, Tom, *Digital Darwinism: Survival of the Fittest in the Age of Business Disruption*, Kogan Page, London, 2018, 10.
4. Shijia, Ouyang, and Chen Jia, 'New Guideline to Better Allocate Production Factors', *China Daily*, April 2020, https://tinyurl.com/394w7rc2. Accessed on 9 December 2022.
5. Barua, Anitesh, Deepa Mani, and Rajiv Mukherjee, 'Measuring the Business Impacts of Effective Data', *The University of Texas at Austin*, https://tinyurl.com/4nj6f2y4. Accessed on 9 December 2022.
6. Lee, Kai-Fu, *AI Superpowers: China, Silicon Valley, and the New World Order*, Houghton Mifflin Harcourt, Boston, MA, 2018.

CHAPTER 2: VISION IN THE DIGITAL WORLD

1. Dyck, Jeremy, 'The Xerox Thieves: Steve Jobs & Bill Gates', *BC Digest*, October 2019, https://tinyurl.com/yc3uzpkp. Accessed on 15 August 2022.
2. Kozlenko, Maksym, 'Xerox Alto Computer', *Wikimedia Commons*, 15 February 2015, https://tinyurl.com/4zmyuhef. Accessed on 11 April 2024.
3. 'Triumph of the Nerds', *All About Steve Jobs*, 2011, https://tinyurl.com/2wd7hbyn. Accessed on 17 November 2024.
4. Dyck, Jeremy, 'The Xerox Thieves: Steve Jobs & Bill Gates', *BC Digest*, October 2019, https://tinyurl.com/yc3uzpkp. Accessed on 9 December 2022.

CHAPTER 3: OUTCOME-BASED BUSINESS MODELS

1. Drab, Emilie, 'How Rolls-Royce is Dealing with the Future Growth in Maintenance Activities', *Le Journal De L'Aviation*, 2017, https://tinyurl.com/558m973d. Accessed on 14 August 2022.
2. 'Uber's India Driver Count Tops 1 Million', *The Economic Times*, 9 May 2024, https://tinyurl.com/5a9ceejv. Accessed on 14 August 2022.
3. The figure has been adapted from the Deloitte analysis; Gill, Jagjeet, Anne Kwan, and Maximilian Schroeck, 'Scaling XaaS: Outcome-based Monetization Models', *Deloitte Insights*, 5 November 2021, https://tinyurl.com/5n89zb6s. Accessed on 15 August 2022.

CHAPTER 4: MEASURE, MONITOR AND IMPROVE

1. Wang, Yifan, Shen Hong, and Crystal Tai, 'China's Efforts to Lead the Way in AI Start in Its Classrooms', *The Wall Street Journal*, October 2019, https://tinyurl.com/mr2hfcyr. Accessed on 19 August 2022.
2. Developed using generative AI.
3. 'Diabetes', *World Health Organization*, https://tinyurl.com/3n9mp27z. Accessed on 6 January 2024.

CHAPTER 5: WORKING WITH MACHINES: AUGMENTED INTELLIGENCE

1. Goodrich, Joanna, 'How IBM's Deep Blue Beat World Champion Chess Player Garry Kasparov', *IEEE Spectrum*, January 2021, https://tinyurl.com/2p9h68s. Accessed on 20 August 2022.
2. Koch, Christof, 'How the Computer Beat the Go Master', *Scientific American*, 19 March 2016, https://tinyurl.com/mrytfrhy. Accessed on 29 January 2023.
3. 'IHC Appoints AI-Powered Virtual Entity Aiden Insight as Board Observer', *ETHRWorld*, 28 February 2024, https://tinyurl.com/c9d6f6mm. Accessed on 11 April 2024.
4. McKinney, Scott Mayer, et al., 'International Evaluation of an AI System for Breast Cancer Screening', *Nature*, 577, 2020, 89–94, https://doi.org/10.1038/s41586-019-1799-6. Accessed on 17 November 2024.
5. Rajalakshmi, Ramachandran, Radhakrishnan Subashini, Ranjit Mohan Anjana, and Viswanathan Mohan, 'Automated Diabetic Retinopathy Detection in Smartphone-based Fundus Photography Using Artificial Intelligence', *Eye*, 2018, https://doi.org/10.1038/s41433-018-0064-9. Accessed on 12 May 2024.
6. 'Chennai Hospital to Use AI to Screen for Glaucoma and Diabetic Retinopathy', *The Hindu*, 12 October 2023, https://tinyurl.com/ycxnk2bp. Accessed on 12 May 2024.
7. Sharma, Harikishan, 'Rs 500 Crore for Namo Drone Didi Scheme, Rs 365 Crore for Natural Farming Mission', *The Indian Express*, 24 July 2024, https://tinyurl.com/mufztrmr. Accessed on 17 November 2024.
8. 'Alarmed by AI Chatbots, Universities Start Revamping How They Teach', *The New York Times*, 16 January 2023, https://tinyurl.com/47ccsac4. Accessed on 17 November 2024.
9. Duarte, Fabio, 'Number of ChatGPT Users', *Exploding Topics*, 5 January 2024, https://tinyurl.com/mvysf77z. Accessed on 7 January 2024.
10. 'Sam Altman Says GPT-5 could be a "Significant Leap Forward", But There's Still "A Lot of Work To Do"', *The Decoder*, 27 June 2024, https://tinyurl.com/d9eu7cv. Accessed on 28 July 2024.

11 'Zarya of the Dawn (Registration #VAu001480196)', *United States Copyright Office*, 21 February 2023, https://tinyurl.com/44avkvc6. Accessed on 2 April 2023.
12 Hougaard, Rasmus, Jacqueline Carter, and Rob Stembridge, 'The Best Leaders Can't Be Replaced by AI', *Harvard Business Review*, 12 January 2024, https://tinyurl.com/52uspd8h. Accessed on 28 July 2024.
13 Ibid. Adapted from the article.

CHAPTER 6: WARY OF BIASES IN DATA

1 Amrein-Beardsley, Audrey, 'VAMboozled!: Houston Lawsuit Update, with Summary of Expert Witnesses' Findings about the EVAAS', National Education Policy Centre (NEPC), *University of Colorado*, 19 January 2016, https://tinyurl.com/3h782wvf. Accessed on 21 August 2022.
2 Angwin, Julia, Jeff Larson, Surya Mattu, and Lauren Kirchner, 'Machine Bias: There's Software Used Across the Country to Predict Future Criminals. And It's Biased Against Blacks', *Propublica*, https://tinyurl.com/muj2phrx. Accessed on 21 August 2022.
3 Ibid.
4 Shin, Terence, 'Real-life Examples of Discriminating Artificial Intelligence', *Towards Data Science*, June 2020, https://tinyurl.com/yawc88bh. Accessed on 21 August 2022.
5 Sen, Anirban, 'When Artificial Intelligence Goes Wrong', *Mint*, August 2017, https://tinyurl.com/3knrs964. Accessed on 21 August 2022.
6 Ghoneim, Salma, '5 Types of Bias & How to Eliminate Them in Your Machine Learning Project', *Towards Data Science*, 16 April 2019, https://tinyurl.com/4hatn72e. Accessed on 28 December 2022.

CHAPTER 7: PROCESS INNOVATION

1 'About Michael Faraday', *Edubilla*, https://tinyurl.com/hw4a77uf. Accessed on 17 November 2024.
2 Wellcome Images, 'Portrait of Michael Faraday (1791–1867)', *Wikimedia Commons*, 24 October 2014, https://tinyurl.com/yr6zyxur. Accessed on 17 November 2024.

3. Bhattacharyya, Rica, and Lijee Philip, 'How India Inc Is Boosting Productivity by Using Intelligent Technologies', *The Economic Times*, 14 January 2024, https://tinyurl.com/yc4kzupx. Accessed on 14 January 2024.
4. Gupta, Ashutosh, 'What Is a Supply Chain Control Tower— And What's Needed to Deploy One?', *Gartner*, 25 March 2022, https://tinyurl.com/5n8xc437. Accessed on 1 January 2023.

CHAPTER 8: CHANGE LEADER: AGILE AND ADAPTABLE

1. 'About George Eastman', *Kodak*, https://tinyurl.com/559xeuw4. Accessed on 27 August 2022.
2. Taneja, Yash, 'Why Did Kodak Fail? | Kodak Bankruptcy Case Study', *Startuptalky*, 6 November 2021, https://tinyurl.com/y4s2b8bf. Accessed on 28 August 2022.
3. 'The Rise and Fall of Blockbuster', *Business Insider India*, 17 January 2020, https://tinyurl.com/muh937e4. Accessed on 28 August 2022.
4. Saini, Leo, 'How Netflix Destroyed Blockbuster in Just 6 Years', *Better Marketing*, 16 November 2019, https://tinyurl.com/bpvpnv6a. Accessed on 28 August 2022.

CHAPTER 9: COOPETITION: AN ECOSYSTEM APPROACH

1. Garbuno, Daniel Martínez, and Molly Russell, 'Codeshare Agreements: Everything You Need To Know', *Simple Flying*, 9 November 2023, https://tinyurl.com/4b5tjp4p. Accessed on 2 January 2023.
2. 'With Us, Digital Farming Is Not a Vision. But Everyday Life', *365FarmNet*, https://www.365farmnet.com/en/. Accessed on 12 September 2022.
3. 'Apple's iPhone 14 Series will have 80% Samsung Display Screens: Report', *Business Standard*, 30 August 2022, https://tinyurl.com/mrx5xd2v. Accessed on 12 September 2022.
4. 'Yahoo and Google Announce New Partnership Deal', *Geek Powered Studios*, 21 October 2015, https://tinyurl.com/3cm47sbm. Accessed on 12 September 2022.

CHAPTER 10: FAKE INFORMATION

1. Dizikes, Peter, 'Study: On Twitter, False News Travels Faster Than True Stories', *MIT News Office*, 8 March 2018, https://tinyurl.com/5ffyeach. Accessed on 10 September 2022.
2. van der Linden, Sander, Jon Roozenbeek, and Josh Compton, 'Inoculating Against Fake News About COVID-19', *Frontiers*, Vol. 11, 2020, https://doi.org/10.3389/fpsyg.2020.566790. Accessed on 10 September 2022.
3. 'Sumsub Research: UK Deepfake Incidents Surge 300% from 2022 to 2023', *PR Newswire*, 28 November 2023, https://tinyurl.com/24rant6x. Accessed on 12 April 2024.
4. 'Creator of Deepfake Video of Actor Rashmika Mandanna Arrested, Says Delhi Police', *The Hindu*, 21 January 2024, https://tinyurl.com/mp378mvz. Accessed on 17 November 2024.
5. Tweet by Sachin Tendulkar, https://tinyurl.com/39b5jry4. Accessed on 16 January 2024.
6. Hassan, Umar, 'Why Fake Data Could be the Biggest Threat to Decision Making', *Tech Monitor*, 18 July 2018, https://tinyurl.com/5dz2aum3. Accessed on 10 September 2022.
7. 'England Schools to Teach How to Spot Online Fake News Under Government Plans', *The Times of India*, 12 August 2024, https://tinyurl.com/yf5v6ues. Accessed on 17 November 2024.
8. McManus, John, 'Don't Be Fooled: Use the SMELL Test to Separate Fact from Fiction Online', *Mediashift.org*, 7 February 2013, https://tinyurl.com/bdd6a58f. Accessed on 3 January 2022.

CHAPTER 11: PERSONALIZATION: THE 5TH P OF MARKETING

1. 'Michael Dell Biography', *Encyclopedia of World Biography*, https://tinyurl.com/cw3sy765. Accessed on 14 September 2022.
2. Duhigg, Charles, 'How Companies Learn Your Secrets', *The New York Times*, 16 February 2012, https://tinyurl.com/yck32va3. Accessed on 17 November 2024.

CHAPTER 12: THE SAFETY OF HUMANS

1. Nair, Sandhya, 'Pandole Booked for Rash Driving, Negligence

in Mistry Accident Case', *The Times of India*, 6 November 2022, https://tinyurl.com/34cvnsuw. Accessed on 6 November 2022.
2. 'Table 2.3: Trends of Major Parameters of Accident by Category of Roads', *Road Accidents in India 2022*, Ministry of Road Transport and Highways (Transport Research Wing), https://tinyurl.com/298jyvsw. Accessed on 28 July 2024.
3. 'What Percentage of Car Accidents Are Caused by Human Error?', *Caroselli, Beachler & Coleman LLC*, 22 September 2021, https://tinyurl.com/273fbp3v. 'NHTSA Releases 2020 Traffic Crash Data', U.S. Department of Transportation, 2 March 2022, https://tinyurl.com/mv9knuex. Both accessed on 9 October 2022.
4. Geere, Duncan, 'Elon Musk: Human Drivers are "Too Dangerous"', *Wired*, 18 March 2015, https://tinyurl.com/2u4uc5vp. Accessed on 9 October 2022.
5. 'Pioneering Automation and Robotics in Mining', *Rio Tinto*, https://tinyurl.com/2z3h6p9e. Accessed on 9 October 2022.

CHAPTER 13: FRAUD DETECTION AND PREVENTION

1. FBI Internet Crime Report 2021, *Internet Crime Complaint Centre*, 4 April 2022, https://tinyurl.com/4kwmvh9j. Accessed on 9 October 2022.
2. Nellis, Stephen, 'Ex-Apple Worker Charged with Stealing Self-Driving Car Trade Secrets', *Reuters*, 11 July 2018, https://tinyurl.com/2mdvyz6y. Accessed on 5 November 2022.

CHAPTER 14: DATA SECURITY

1. Kerner, Sean Michael, 'Colonial Pipeline Hack Explained: Everything You Need to Know', *Techtarget*, 26 April 2022, https://tinyurl.com/2f6u26tc. Accessed on 8 November 2022.
2. Whitehead, Sam, 'Colonial Pipeline System', *Wikimedia Commons*, 12 May 2021, https://tinyurl.com/p5yem4t6. Accessed on 10 February 2024.
3. Falconer, Rebecca, 'Emergency Declaration Issued in 17 States and D.C. Over Fuel Pipeline Cyberattack', *Axios*, 10 May 2021, https://tinyurl.com/2jm88r2. Accessed on 8 November 2022.

4 'Danish Train Standstill on Saturday Caused by Cyber Attack', *Reuters*, 4 November 2022, https://tinyurl.com/4v68c5uc. Accessed on 4 January 2023.

5 Kumar, Ayush, 'AIIMS Ransomware Attack: The Missing Picture', *News18*, 20 December 2022, https://tinyurl.com/3tu95srx. Accessed on 4 January 2023.

6 'AIIMS Data Retrieved, Services Restored: Govt', *India Today*, 16 December 2022, https://tinyurl.com/5f64bzb6. Accessed on 4 January 2023.

7 Greenberg, Andy, 'The Untold Story of NotPetya, the Most Devastating Cyberattack in History', *The Wired*, 22 August 2018, https://tinyurl.com/ytzv7t94. Accessed on 28 July 2024.

8 Morgan, Steve, 'Cybercrime to Cost the World $10.5 Trillion Annually by 2025', *Cybercrime Magazine*, 13 November 2020, https://tinyurl.com/b5jt8r57. Accessed on 8 November 2022.

9 Cobb, Michael, 'How to Perform a Cybersecurity Risk Assessment in 5 Steps', *Techtarget*, 18 January 2024, https://tinyurl.com/yued397w. Accessed on 8 November 2022.

10 Buckbee, Michael, 'Analyzing Company Reputation After a Data Breach', *Varonis*, 29 March 2020, https://tinyurl.com/2j85657v. Accessed on 4 January 2023.

CHAPTER 15: EMOTIONAL INTELLIGENCE

1 Michels, Madeline, 'Crying Wolf? Project RYaN, US Intelligence, and the 1983 "War Scare"', *Wilson Center*, 2 September 2020, https://tinyurl.com/3rr9mk3e. Accessed on 26 November 22.

2 'About Pershing II', *US National Air and Space Museum*, https://tinyurl.com/2cav94eh. Accessed on 26 November 22.

3 'Korean Air Lines Flight 007: Air Disaster Near Sakhalin Island, Russia [1983]', *Britannica*, https://tinyurl.com/3kwk5rrz. Accessed on 26 November 22.

4 'The Night the World Almost Ended', *BBC Global*, YouTube, 9 January 2020, https://tinyurl.com/yrvz5nte. Accessed on 26 November 2022.

5 Aksenov, Pavel, 'Stanislav Petrov: The Man Who May Have Saved the World', *BBC Russian*, 26 September 2013, https://tinyurl.com/3r83xvkr. Accessed on 26 November 2022.

6 Gray, Alex, 'The 10 Skills You Need to Thrive in the Fourth Industrial Revolution', *World Economic Forum*, 19 January 2016, https://tinyurl.com/yaw8b7mr. Accessed on 26 November 2022.

7 Pekaar, Keri A., Dimitri van der Linden, Arnold B. Bakker, and Marise Ph. Born, 'Emotional Intelligence and Job Performance: The Enactment and Focus on Others' Emotions', *Human Performance*, Vol. 30, Nos. 2–3, 2017, 135–153, https://doi.org/10.1080/08959285.2017.1332630. Accessed on 17 November 2024.

CHAPTER 16: HORIZONTAL ORGANIZATIONAL STRUCTURE

1 Goss, Jennifer L., 'Henry Ford and the Auto Assembly Line', *Thoughtco.*, 22 January 2020, https://tinyurl.com/57vmxfsp. Accessed on 27 November 2022.

2 Fountaine, Tim, Brian McCarthy, and Tamim Saleh, 'Building the AI-Powered Organization-Technology Isn't the Biggest Challenge. Culture Is', *Harvard Business Review*, July–August 2019, https://tinyurl.com/msz5fmp8. Accessed on 27 November 2022.

3 'Millennials at Work: Reshaping the Workplace', *PwC*, 25 March 2013, https://tinyurl.com/47y8xbfh. Accessed on 17 November 2024.

CHAPTER 17: THE FUTURE OF WORK: WORK 5.0

1 Kopf, Dan, 'Slowly but Surely, Working at Home Is Becoming More Common', *Quartz*, 17 September 2018, https://tinyurl.com/3tam3c88. Accessed on 10 February 2024.

2 Kuhnke, Elizabeth, 'Defining Body Language', *Body Language For Dummies*, John Wiley & Sons, West Sussex, 2015, 12, https://tinyurl.com/7rub2k4e. Accessed on 10 February 2024.

3 Created by the author using generative AI

CHAPTER 18: HUMAN RESOURCE MANAGEMENT

1 'A knocker-up in Leeuwarden, 1947', *Nationaal Archief*, 15 February 2009, https://tinyurl.com/bde7py2z; 'Before There Were Alarm Clocks, Knocker-Ups Were Paid to Wake Up Their Clients by Knocking!', *Vintage Everyday*, 21 July 2019, https://tinyurl.com/39kakj7n. Both accessed on 10 February 2024.

2. 'Work/Life Balance at Intel', *intel*, https://tinyurl.com/mr452p2p. Accessed on 6 January 2023.
3. Manyika, James, Susan Lund, Jacques Bughin, Kelsey Robinson, Jan Mischke, and Deepa Mahajan, 'Independent Work: Choice, Necessity, and the Gig Economy', *McKinsey Global Institute*, 10 October 2016, https://tinyurl.com/e67yb854. Accessed on 17 November 2024.

CHAPTER 19: PREDICTIVE ANALYTICS AND DEMAND FORECASTING

1. Tuthill, Kathleen, 'John Snow and the Broad Street Pump', *Cricket*, Vol. 31, No. 3, 2003, 23–31, https://tinyurl.com/2zzx59dr. Accessed on 3 December 2022.
2. 'John Snow—The Father of Epidemiology', *Boston University School of Public Health*, https://tinyurl.com/555uchpk. Accessed on 3 December 2022.
3. Snow, John, *On the Mode of Communication of Cholera*, C.F. Cheffins, Lithograph, London, 1854, https://tinyurl.com/mrzfa5bu. Accessed on 17 November 2024 and modified to highlight certain items.
4. Stieg, Cory, 'How this Canadian Start-Up Spotted Coronavirus Before Everyone Else Knew About It', *CNBC*, 6 March 2020, https://tinyurl.com/yfyykht2. Accessed on 8 June 2023.
5. 'What is Predictive Analytics?', *IBM*, https://tinyurl.com/3v238sfy. Accessed on 3 December 2022.
6. 'Maximum Uptime, All The Time', *ThyssenKrupp*, 22 April 2020, https://tinyurl.com/2n53bps2. Accessed on 17 November 2024.

CHAPTER 20: RESPONSIBLE AI

1. Sterling, Bruce, 'Chinese Planning Outlining for a Social Credit System', *Wired*, 3 June 2015, https://tinyurl.com/y6bs3wwf. Accessed on 4 December 2022.
2. 'China's "Social Credit" System', *Artificial Intelligence*, 16 September 2022, https://tinyurl.com/4zc7y5fm. Accessed on 4 December 2022.
3. 'China's Latest AI Chatbot is Trained on President Xi Jinping's Political Ideology', *The Times of India*, 24 May 2024, https://tinyurl.com/57jncv6p. Accessed on 27 May 2024.

4 'Responsible AI: Scale AI with Confidence', *Accenture*, https://tinyurl.com/4jtec8j7. Accessed on 4 December 2022.
5 Mills, Steven, Elias Baltassis, Maximiliano Santinelli, Cathy Carlisi, Sylvian Duranton, and Andrea Gallego, 'Six Steps to Bridge the Responsible AI Gap', *Boston Consulting Group*, 8 September 2020, https://tinyurl.com/mry75rv6. Accessed on 4 December 2022.

CHAPTER 21: DATA QUALITY AND GOVERNANCE

1 Little, Becky, 'Christa McAuliffe: How NASA's Teacher in Space Project Ended in Tragedy', *History*, 15 April 2024, https://tinyurl.com/5x84jztj. Accessed on 24 April 2024.
2 'Rogers Commission Report', *NASA*, 6 June 1986, https://tinyurl.com/2p99c3t. Accessed on 9 January 2023.
3 Ibid. Reproduced Figure 6 from the Rogers Commission Report, p. 147.
4 Ibid. Reproduced Figure 7 from the Rogers Commission Report, p. 147.
5 Ibid. 146. Italicized by the author for emphasis.
6 Uppenkamp, Max, 'Data Quality Disasters', *Informadatalab*, 6 October 2020, https://tinyurl.com/4u5bw7ed. Accessed on 9 January 2023.
7 'Mars Climate Orbiter Mishap Investigation Board Phase I Report, *NASA*, 10 November 1999, https://tinyurl.com/mte8dzzz. Accessed on 10 January 2023.
8 Ibid. Reproduced Figure 4 from the Mars Climate Orbiter Mishap Investigation Board Phase I Report, p. 14.
9 Here, two examples have been taken from NASA to emphasize the value of data quality. There is absolutely no intention to discredit NASA's achievements in space exploration.

CHAPTER 22: THE BLUE SCREEN CATASTROPHE

1 'Blue Screen of Death', *Wikimedia Commons*, 30 October 2022, https://tinyurl.com/52nh9czm. Accessed on 28 July 2024.
2 Anchil, Juviraj, '₹4,185 Crore Outage: Microsoft Tech Glitch Hit Airlines, Banks & Healthcare The Hardest, Says Report', *The Free*

Press Journal, 25 July 2024, https://tinyurl.com/287vcpps. Accessed on 27 July 2024.
3. 'CrowdStrike Preliminary Post Incident Review Executive Summary', *CrowdStrike*, 24 July 2024, https://tinyurl.com/38z2kku7. Accessed on 28 July 2024.

CHAPTER 23: DIGITAL TRANSFORMATION

1. Jolly, Damian, 'What Amazon can Teach Us about Digital Transformation in Manufacturing', *Nukon*, 28 September 2017, https://tinyurl.com/mat3b3km. Accessed on 28 May 2023.
2. 'Creation of GE Digital', *General Electric Company*, 14 September 2015, https://tinyurl.com/4xwxjcut. Accessed on 28 May 2023.